STUDYING PART TIME WITHOUT STRESS

By the same author:

Studying in Australia: A guide for international students

STUDYING PART TIME WITHOUT STRESS

Teresa De Fazio

ALLEN&UNWIN

To Gib and my children

First published in 2002

Allen & Unwin
83 Alexander Street
Crows Nest NSW 2065
Australia
Phone: (61 2) 8425 0100
Fax: (61 2) 9906 2218
Email: info@allenandunwin.com
Web: www.allenandunwin.com

National Library of Australia
Cataloguing-in-Publication entry:

De Fazio, Teresa.
    Studying part time without stress.

    Bibliography.
    Includes index.
    ISBN 1 86508 646 0.

    1. Study skills. 2. Students, Part-time—Time management.
    I. Title

378.17028

Set in 11/13 Adobe Garamond by Midland Typesetters, Maryborough, Victoria
Printed by McPherson's Printing Group, Maryborough, Victoria

10 9 8 7 6 5 4 3 2 1

Contents

Acknowledgments

I am grateful to the students I have worked with over the years who have provided me with wonderful models for the role I now find myself in, juggling family, work, writing and study.

I thank my family for their faithful support and the good humour that helps keep me sane, my mother for her assistance, and Elizabeth Weiss, Gillian Markham, Karen Penning and others at Allen & Unwin for their assistance and confidence in this project.

Introduction

Contrary to the perception held up until the last twenty years or so that education took up only a particular stage of life (generally the years between the ages of 5 and 25), education is now being seen as a continuous activity. Tertiary institutions are responding to this shift in perception by providing a range of formal courses that can be accessed day or evening, full time or part time, and designed to suit various students through flexible learning programs.

As a part-time student you will probably not have the luxury of devoting your time entirely to study, instead juggling study, relationships, work, parenthood, social life, community responsibility or some other interest. It's hardly surprising if you sometimes stop and wonder how on Earth you can possibly stay sane! This book is relevant to all those who, for whatever reason, wish to undertake part-time studies. It is intended to help you think about yourself as a student and to develop the sorts of skills and knowledge base that will help you become an effective learner, rather than losing your self and your time as you become swamped by the whole academic experience. It is about understanding and enjoying the process of learning rather than just reaching the practical outcomes of a study experience. It explores the academic environment and its requirements of you, suggests strategies, gives hints and explains processes that will enable you to feel equipped as you slip into the scholarly world and out again into your other worlds.

The book is written from the perspective of years of teaching experience, and also from a personal perspective, as I now find myself juggling studies with a career and a new family (in fact, as I write this paragraph I have dinner and the washing machine on the go, a baby tucked up in bed, building plans waiting for attention, a lecture to prepare and a literature review to redraft). Studying part time should not be a new take on being superman or superwoman, however.

A major theme explored throughout this book is the idea of entering into academic argument. As part of your studies you are required to take an active role in the process of reasoning to come to certain conclusions. Reasoning is demonstrated through such aspects as your written work, class discussions, projects, reading, exams and so on. Tertiary education is not just a series of fragmented classes and assignments (though at times it may seem this way); it is a process of discovery and knowledge development and acquiring critical skills.

Gaining familiarity with your university or college environment is the focus of the first chapter. The aim is to facilitate the information-seeking process so that you will select the right course and then organise it to suit your study purpose. The next chapter takes this a step further in terms of preparing yourself to take up the role of part-time student, both mentally, by exploring learning styles, critical reasoning processes and skills development, and physically, by organising your environment to enable you to pursue your study objectives. In Chapter 3 we turn to the practical aspect of time management and how to organise a busy schedule so that the study experience does not turn out to be a stressful one. Chapter 4 takes up the issue of critical reasoning and how it is demonstrated through participation in the different types of classes you may encounter during your study experience. This chapter also explores giving oral presentations as part of class participation.

Note-taking is part of both class participation and the reading process. Chapter 5 investigates these aspects of study and provides strategies for dealing with what can be a lot of complex reading material. Chapters 6 to 9 deal with developing an understanding of the writing process and developing the sense of argument that should underly any written text. While Chapter 6 explores general writing processes and techniques, Chapter 7 looks at essay writing in particular and provides a worked example. The next chapter reviews report writing while Chapter 9 outlines the three major referencing conventions: Harvard, Footnote/Endnote and APA. Chapter 10 reviews exam preparation and effective strategies for dealing with exams on the day. The next chapter is dedicated to research projects, which can be quite demanding in terms of thinking, organisation and presentation. Chapter 12 deals with the use of technological tools as part of your studies, including e-mail, the Internet and electronic databases; it also details strategies that will help you exploit these tools without wasting a lot of time and effort in dealing with technology for technology's sake.

To gain a broad view of the information you need, it would be helpful to read the entire book first. As you progress in your studies, you can refer back to the separate chapters and the guides in the appendices section as you need to.

I hope that those of you who are about to embark on part-time studies will find that this book helps to demystify some of the issues surrounding academia and facilitates your learning experience. I wish you well in your studies and hope you find this book as enjoyable to use as I found to write.

1

Choosing to study part time

Universities and colleges are becoming more responsive to training, vocational and commercial factors and offer a broader range of courses and delivery modes than a few years ago. Colleges and universities can seem rather daunting in terms of the number of departments, information services, student support services and other aspects that make up study life. This chapter looks at issues in navigating through the system to make it work for you. It outlines course delivery modes and the kinds of support offered. Knowing how the academic system works will ensure that you make effective use of your time and energy.

CHOOSING TO STUDY

Before you commit yourself to studying part time you need to carefully consider the reason behind your decision in terms of what you want to achieve. You may be motivated to study for practical reasons—for a promotion or to expand your work opportunities.

You may be determined to study because you have never had the opportunity before and want to prove you can do it. It might be that pure interest and a desire to learn more about a discipline are driving you. Your motivation may be a combination of work-oriented reasons and personal interest. Certainly, having a healthy interest in the subjects you choose helps to maintain the motivation levels to get through what might be a number of years devoted to study, although some students do very well when driven to study purely as a means to a work-related end. While there is no right or wrong reason for studying, keeping in mind the rationale behind undertaking a course will help you maintain focus. The checklist below may help you identify your underlying reasons.

✓ **CHECKLIST: REASONS FOR CHOOSING TO STUDY**

❏ To learn about a particular topic

❏ To upgrade my skills

❏ To upgrade my qualifications

❏ To meet others in my field

❏ To widen my area of interests

❏ To learn or sharpen my study skills

❏ To extend my intellectual interests and skills

❏ To prove to myself I can do it

❏ To prove to others I can do it

❏ To make new friends

❏ To get a promotion

❏ To widen my work opportunities

CHOOSING A COURSE

Once you have considered your reasons for taking up study you are in a better position to work out your study pathway. If you want to study purely for interest's sake, it might not matter that you take a sprinkling of courses in different disciplines, say languages, biomedicine, chemistry and dramatic arts. If you are motivated by vocational or further educational purposes then you should consider arranging your pathway so that the course and subjects you select provide you with the skills and knowledge (and perhaps networks) you need to pursue your objectives.

There are a huge number of courses available from numerous academic institutions. Through distance learning programs you may select a course in another part of the country or even overseas. With so much choice the selection process can be rather difficult. Below is a checklist to help you ascertain the best course for you.

✓ CHECKLIST: CHOOSING THE RIGHT COURSE

❑ Do you know what the course involves? You need to do more than just read the title and brief description provided in the course handbook or leaflet. Talk to the course co-ordinator about the topics covered, previous study or experience required, assessment tasks and set reading.

❑ Do the subjects interest you? Are they of value to your study objectives?

❑ Do the subjects make up a solid program that will assist you on your study pathway?

❑ Will you be able to gain any credits towards the completion of the course as a result of past studies or experience in the field? (*See* Recognition of prior learning on p. 9)

❑ Do you need to take any preparatory courses? You might consider taking a summer school course if you have no experience with a particular subject; for instance, if you are doing a postgraduate course which involves research you might choose to do an introductory research methodology course during the summer months. You should talk to the course coordinator regarding the need to undertake preparatory courses.

Using handbooks

Institutional handbooks provide a useful outline of the courses offered and the topics covered in each course. If the topics are not detailed in the handbook it might be worthwhile contacting the course coordinator to find out more. Most lecturers or course coordinators will be able to provide you with a more detailed outline and answer questions regarding preparatory reading, assessment and entry requirements. Handbooks also explain the different degree programs and entry requirements, institutional regulations and particular study options you may wish to take up, such as distance mode, flexible mode, recognition of prior learning, return-to-study programs and so on. Handbooks can be purchased from the institutional bookshop or may be consulted in the library. Course information is usually available online as well. Most institutions will have their handbooks or course outlines available from a link on their homepage.

CHOOSING YOUR SUBJECTS

Every course is made up of a number of subjects. In some courses you must take every prescribed subject, in others you have many options. The subjects must be selected carefully, according to your study purpose and interests. Some might be very appealing in terms of their content and your personal interests, but consider their practicality for your purposes, and the demands on your time—the scheduling of classes, the number of classes you need to attend, the delivery mode (distance or face-to-face), assessment requirements and so on. You might be tempted to do a number of interesting but rather demanding subjects in one year or semester. A knowledge of the practical aspects involved may suggest it would be better to stagger them over a longer period.

FLEXIBLE LEARNING PROGRAMS

Undertaking a flexible learning program means that you do not necessarily have to undertake a course according to a rigid, systematic pathway but can choose, within reason, to customise a course to suit your study situation and study purposes. These days interdisciplinary study programs are quite common, that is, programs that do not lock you into taking, for instance, a strict business course. Instead you may take integrated studies that include units on psychology and a language as well as business-oriented subjects. Depending on previous experience and study you may not have to undertake every unit in the course (*see* Recognition of prior learning, below). You might be able to undertake units either in semester breaks or during intensive sessions held during summer or winter breaks. Every institution has different policies regarding the flexibility of a program, and this aspect is worth looking into.

DISTANCE LEARNING

Many tertiary institutions offer subjects or whole courses by distance. This might mean that documents are sent out to you by mail, or that you can access subject information over the Internet, or a combination of the two. Some institutions arrange for local tutors to be available to assist with tasks and assignments. As technology is integrated into education, different equipment is coming into use; for instance, some lectures are held via video-conferencing. It is important to clarify how the subjects are organised if you are thinking of taking up a course by distance education. Ask about what you can expect in terms of learning materials, assistance with tasks, access to lecturers, the sort of services you have access to (library, study groups, etc.) and the equipment you will need. Importantly, consider whether the distance mode suits you. Are you good at working alone, for instance, or do you need the stimulus of face-to-face interaction?

RECOGNITION OF PRIOR LEARNING

Recognition of prior learning (RPL) is a process by which you can obtain credit towards a degree for past courses or subjects studied, or for relevant work experience. You need to provide evidence of such studies or experience: certificates you have been awarded or a statement of results, or a letter from your employer that outlines the duties in which you are involved. You may be credited with equivalent points instead of actually undertaking all or part of a subject.

ENROLLING, WITHDRAWING, DEFERRING

Student expectations of the value of a course may not match its reality. It is always worth asking about the cut-off date for withdrawing from a course; if you leave it too late you may find that a fail result appears on your academic records instead of a witdrawal. Sometimes it is not possible to continue studying a subject because of illness, family responsibilities or a change in your work situation. Talk to your lecturer about your circumstances to see if there is any way of salvaging the situation (late submission of work, for instance). Otherwise it is worth deferring a subject or withdrawing from the whole course rather than failing completely (again check for the cut-off date). Disappearing from a course and then re-appearing can be rather confusing so let the lecturer(s) involved know that you intend to resume studies at a later date.

FINANCING YOUR STUDIES

Scholarships and bursaries are a way of easing the financial burden of studying. They may be funded by various institutions as well as by the educational institution itself—for instance, community groups such as Rotary, and pharmaceutical companies. Tertiary institution websites have information on general and institutional scholarships and grants or check with the student services officer or postgraduate officer at the institution in which you are enrolled (or will enrol) for details. If you find that financing your studies becomes difficult, rather than dropping out speak to someone in student services; there may be some assistance available in the form of student loans.

SUPPORT SERVICES

Most tertiary institutions provide a number of student support services and you should never feel embarrassed about accessing them. They are there because there is a need.

Learning support

Seek guidance from learning support advisors. They are there to help *all* students, not just students with second-language problems (as is sometimes believed). Even students who are doing well in their studies find that some tasks are difficult—exam preparation, for instance, reading skills or essay planning. It is important to get guidance on study issues that are concerning you.

Disability support

The disability support office is there to provide guidance and assistance on services for students with disabilities. Make contact with this office to find out what services your institution provides in regard to facilities, equipment and policies to help you get the most out of your study experience.

Student counselling

This service offers a range of support and guidance on such things as time management and stress management, finances and tax issues, student concessions, sexual harassment and racism. You will find helpful advice as well as counsellors and psychologists to assist you in getting back on track or to deal with any such problems.

Equity services

Equity services provide advice and assistance on equity and discrimination issues. Should you have a complaint or simply want information the service officers will be able to guide you on managing and dealing with the issue, particularly in terms of the institutional policies and procedures on such matters.

Health centre

Every institution provides some medical care. Often both a doctor and nurse are employed to attend to the medical requirements of the academic community. Some institutions also provide optometry, dentistry and physiotherapy. The cost may be covered by government public health care benefits.

Financial services

This service provides both advice and loan schemes customised to suit the needs of students. It is worth seeking help on financial issues which may be affecting your academic progress.

Accommodation

Student services offer a housing service for students to assist in locating rental housing or purchasing property. It also offers lots of practical advice on dealing with real estate agents and lessors, and can assist with any legal issues.

Indigenous student office

This service offers support and guidance specifically for indigenous students. This may include assisting with relocation, facilitating contact with other students, orientation, social and study programs.

Religious services

A chaplaincy is normally available, regardless of religious affiliation, to offer support and advice to students in need. Student groups representing a range of religious faiths often arrange information, social and religious activities on campus.

Employment services

Employment services normally list job vacancies available to students. These can range from part-time casual factory jobs to full-time professional positions for graduates. Such a service may also arrange industry-related information and interview sessions. Advice on interview techniques and preparation of job-seeking documents is also available.

LIBRARY SERVICES

The two main sources of academic information are institutional libraries and the Internet. To use each source appropriately requires familiarity with its functions and what it has to offer. (Chapter 12 concentrates on using the Internet as an information source.) Your academic library will probably be the foremost source of helpful information. Lecturers will inform the library of the texts, journals and other information required specifically for their subjects, which makes it easier for you to access materials. Professional libraries are also helpful for specialised information; for instance, an Institute of Engineers' library would stock a variety of information in the form of manuals, journals and reports and may be able to help with information on standards. Municipal libraries can also be helpful, not only for information but also by providing a quiet study atmosphere close to home when you need to get away to concentrate. Librarians will assist with information on how their library functions and on accessing information, even if the information needs to be sourced elsewhere.

University libraries hold a lot more than books and journals these days so it is worthwhile making the effort early on to get to know what materials and equipment are available. One way of doing this is to book into a library tour. These are normally arranged at the beginning of each semester and may be a general tour or a tour specifically booked for your class by your lecturer. (*See also* Using the library, p. 69)

Choosing to study, for whatever reason, results in a significant commitment of time and energy so it is important to consider what you want and need from your course, and to investigate what different institutions offer in terms of course content and student support. The study process should be beneficial not only in terms of the scholarly knowledge you will develop, but in the skills that will enrich your outlook and general life experience.

> **What we have to learn to do, we learn by doing.**
>
> Aristotle

2

Yourself as learner and critical thinker

When you choose to undertake tertiary studies, particularly if you have not studied for some time, at some point you are bound to end up questioning your readiness to take up the challenge; you may even be concerned about your role as a student. This is natural. Even those who have already undertaken tertiary study feel nervous about taking up studies at a higher level. Having a sense of your natural strengths and abilities will stand you in good stead and allow you to deal with such issues as the development of new skills, changes in direction and flagging motivation. This chapter discusses a number of aspects that will help in reflecting on yourself as a learner, facilitate your preparation and boost your confidence.

JUGGLING WORK, STUDY AND LIFE

Juggling relationships, home, work, a social life and study will probably be the biggest challenge you ever face, but you will relish the feeling of satisfaction (and relief) when you finally graduate. By planning and organising your activities, coopting the assistance of those around you and keeping an eye out for stress indicators, you will be better able to study productively without losing too much of yourself in the process. An important step in your preparation for the study process is to examine your support networks: consider your partner, family, friends, work environment, the institution where you are enrolled and, of course, your *self*. How much support for your studies can you expect from each of these sources?

RECRUITING THE ASSISTANCE OF YOUR PARTNER AND FAMILY

Choosing to study part time usually means choosing to deal with an extra role and an extra workload. Balancing everything gets to be a tricky series of manoeuvres. It is important, therefore, to recruit the assistance of your partner and family. This will mean explaining your decision to ensure that your studies and their value to you are understood and respected. It is important to make clear what your studies will lead to—better job prospects, for instance, or a personal sense of fulfilment. Discuss all the ways that each of you sees life changing. Your partner and children may realise that you will be unable to do all the things you used to do. Give them the opportunity to explain how they feel about the changes, as unexpressed resentment can lead to all sorts of tensions. They may feel 'discarded', which may make *you* feel guilty. Explain that while the studies will be for a limited time, their support during this time is crucial. Perhaps you could point out how important mutual support and assistance are to the whole dynamics of relationships in life and this is a time when you need to call upon their help. With your partner or family, work out ways in which they can help you physically, by taking over some of the chores and respecting your study time, and emotionally, by being supportive. It may take a few discussions and there may be bumps along the way as new challenges present themselves, but your partner's and family's understanding and support are essential if you are to maintain a positive attitude to your studies.

Invite your partner and children along to visit the institution where you will be studying—open days provide a good opportunity to see what happens and ask questions or just get a sense of the learning environment. Perhaps you could invite them to sit in on a class or go to the library with you one afternoon. Practical ways of involving them so that they become familiar with where you are and what you are doing will assist them in understanding the sort of commitment required of you, and the support you need from them.

Don't forget to thank your partner and family for their support along the way. Plan an activity so that you can all spend time together or bring home a favourite treat, and affirm how much you have appreciated their support.

If no support is forthcoming or your partner or family seem wary of the commitment your studies entail, you may need to persevere in a quietly determined manner on your own. If there is still no change your motivational and organisational powers will be called upon, as well as your ability to deal with any stress that may result. The intent of this book is to provide you with strategies that will help you realise your study objectives without undue stress.

RECRUITING THE SUPPORT OF YOUR WORK COLLEAGUES

Many students find that their employers and colleagues are supportive of their studies. You may even be allotted some study time as part of your week's duties and be given time off for exams. You may be assigned a workplace mentor who can support you, both in terms of discussing course topics or study issues and in keeping you focused (and motivated if need be). A group of colleagues studying similar subjects could even form a study group (see Chapter 4) to meet weekly or fortnightly to discuss issues arising from reading or classes.

On the other hand, you may find that your employer or manager is suspicious rather than supportive. In this case it is important to explain the benefits and your interests clearly. Communicating openly about the value of the course, both for the work environment and for you personally, may ease tensions and dispel any insecurity felt by those around you. This might take some time. Some students find that once their workplace sees some benefits flowing back into the work environment there is a change of attitude for the better. For others it is a matter of 'going it alone', even to the point of saying nothing at work of study plans; these students need to draw extra strength from themselves and from partners, friends and family.

RECRUITING THE ASSISTANCE OF FRIENDS

Your friends will often be very supportive, especially when they understand your objectives and are aware of the obstacles you face. However, you may also find that some friends become uneasy about possible changes to established relationships, fearing that the rapport you share will change as the pursuit of tertiary studies 'leaves them behind'. It is important to discuss any such issues openly as soon as they arise, just as you would discuss any issue that might affect a friendship. You will be busier, with less time to socialise than before, but friends who understand your situation are more likely to be supportive. However, do find some time to socialise and thank your friends for their support. Good friendships are important and need as much nurturing as your study objectives. Finding a balance where you can do both well can be tricky but is worth the effort.

KEEPING MOTIVATION LEVELS UP

Inevitably there will be low periods, when study becomes a burden and you doubt your purpose, agonise over the repercussions of your commitment on those around you, and wonder whether you are 'cut out' for study anyhow. It is important to do things that maintain your sense of focus and keep your motivation levels high. At the start of Chapter 1 we looked at identifying your reasons for study. Write these reasons down on a sheet of coloured paper and pin it above your desk. You might need to refresh your memory when times get tough and your sense of direction goes adrift. You will need to be your own personal trainer or motivator to keep yourself going through the periods when study seems to be all hard work and you cannot see the light at the end of the tunnel.

Sometimes having a mentor can be a great source of support. This mentor may be someone in the workplace or one of your friends. Another source of inspiration might be found in a role model. Thinking about an athlete, a scholar or some other person you admire in terms of how they strove to realise their aims might help in remembering that turning goals into achievements takes effort and persistence.

Take time to celebrate your achievements. When you have completed a task (say, submitting an assignment on time), stop and enjoy that feeling of achievement and treat yourself to some time doing something you enjoy—perhaps a game of tennis or going to a movie. Share the achievement with your partner, family, friends or colleagues—this way you can thank them by celebrating together, and at the same time recruit their ongoing support. This is all part of enjoying the study experience.

Affirmations are often seen as the kitsch side of pop psychology, but they have been an important part of self-motivation for a long time. Where would your favourite sportsperson or mountain-climber Sir Edmund Hillary be without a little self-encouragement? Keep up your motivation levels by repeating an appropriate affirmation to yourself, particularly on difficult days.

USEFUL AFFIRMATIONS

- I know I can, if I think I can.
- I am a good writer (reader, student, etc.).
- I enjoy the challenge of essay writing.
- I am learning to read faster.
- I am learning to write better.
- It's okay if I make mistakes.
- I am learning to organise myself better.

Learn to recognise self-sabotaging strategies. These can include consistently missing lectures, missing assignment deadlines, not completing tasks, not doing important reading, going late to class, simply feeling 'flat' all the time, trying to convince yourself that you are not cut out for studies. The reasons your motivation levels flag may include feeling that you should not really succeed or that you do not fit in to academic life; when these thoughts take hold it is easy to lose direction or become confused about your objectives. If you find you are unable to get motivated on your own or with the assistance of people around you, consider speaking to a student counsellor. Counsellors are trained to help you regain a sense of balance and direction.

AVOIDING STRESS DURING YOUR STUDIES

Avoiding stress completely is probably an unattainable ideal. However, it is important to be able to read your situation and know when you are starting to stress out—and to do something about it. Working quickly to break a stress cycle means you will continue to use your energy effectively.

Sometimes you can feel the stress levels increase because of all the roles you have to fill at work or at home and still keep up the studying. Keep things in perspective. First write a list of the things you have to do—everything. It may end up quite long. Now review your list realistically. Delete the things you will not be able to do. Some things will just have to be done without your involvement, others simply not done at all. The next step is to reduce your workload as much as possible. If there are too many things to do take some short cuts and keep your cool. Don't feel guilty. If you were planning a family birthday banquet at home, for example, reorganise it so that you go out to a restaurant, have a BYO picnic or get takeaway. The next step is to prioritise what must be done immediately and what can wait. Decide when you can realistically complete a task rather than when you would prefer to get it done. Look at the list again. Work out what can be done by someone else—this is where your partner, family, friends and work colleagues can be of support. By prioritising you can enlist assistance and establish realistic deadlines. By the end of this exercise you should feel that you are in control again and can get back on track *doing* rather than *fretting*.

A relaxation strategy

At those times when anxiety builds up, as it inevitably will, practising a simple relaxation exercise can be of great assistance. You might be feeling overwhelmed by the number of things you have to do, feel unsupported (which might also result in feeling isolated) or have other matters to deal with such as relationship or work problems. Anxiety might also overtake you in the face of assignments, reading or exams. Try this simple but effective relaxation strategy. Settle yourself into a comfortable chair (perhaps with relaxation music playing in the background), close your eyes and take three deep slow breaths, focusing on relaxing with each breath. Push away any anxiety with each slow exhalation.

Continue to breathe in and out slowly, relaxing all your muscles, releasing the tension around your forehead, down your neck and shoulders. Continue to focus on parts of your body until you have relaxed all your muscles. Sit quietly for five minutes, breathing slowly and freeing yourself of all that stress. Spending just five or ten minutes in this way will allow you to refocus clearly.

A focusing technique

This focusing technique is also worth learning. Once you are feeling relaxed, using the relaxation strategy, picture yourself undertaking a study task you are currently finding difficult—listening and note-taking in lectures, for instance, preparing for an exam or writing a paper. Try to use all your senses to see yourself holding your note pad, feeling the weight of the pen in your hand, hearing the lecturer's message. Most importantly, picture yourself working away confidently. For a few minutes hold the image in your mind, hold onto the feeling of being in control. You might finish with an affirmation such as 'I am progressing well with this report' or some confident self-talk such as 'I have planned this essay and will be able to write it up'. This is not a new strategy; it has been used in fields such as sport for many years to help athletes focus effectively on their task, regain a sense of control and feel less anxious. It may take a little practice to develop this focusing technique, particularly if you are not a strongly visual person, but it is worth the effort.

STUDY SHOCK

Students often describe going through a period of low motivation, disorientation and loss of focus. Stepping onto campus grounds can feel like stepping onto the moon; nothing around you makes sense or makes you feel as if you belong. I call this *study shock*, because it is almost like culture shock. It is a normal part of orienting oneself to a new situation to find that a long-held direction or dream seems to have gone slightly askew. The first coping strategy here is to remind yourself that this *is* a normal feeling. The academic environment can often seem alienating at first. The expectations of lecturers may be different to what you imagined, or even totally unclear. You are required to do a lot of intensive thinking during classes, usually in one-hour blocks. There is a lot of self-responsibility and sometimes very little guidance in terms of understanding the learning process, developing your own learning skills and feeling comfortable with the academic environment. You are also expected to read a lot, write a lot, listen a lot and (depending on the course) speak a lot of sensible stuff on topics that are covered so quickly that you may feel you have barely understood the material. And the list goes on.

There may be times when you find all this so overwhelming that you lose focus and confidence. This can happen during the ordinary course of your studies, be triggered by a difficult assignment or even overtake you in the middle of an exam or class. You may find yourself thinking, 'This doesn't feel right, I am not meant to be a student', 'This is just too hard, I can't understand anything', even 'Other students must be more intelligent because they seem to be coping better than I am'. These feelings are quite natural, but they should be seen as signals that it is time to refocus rather than time to give up. You may be putting too much pressure on yourself, resulting in difficulty sleeping, falling levels of motivation and confidence, increasing irritability and moodiness. When this happens try the relaxation strategy mentioned above and build in the focusing technique. If you feel really low, speak to someone who will understand—your partner, a colleague, a fellow student—someone who can relate to your situation. If this doesn't help, you should certainly talk to one of your lecturers or a student counsellor. It is important that you talk it out rather than let yourself lose focus and give up. The depression revealed in the remark 'I don't care what marks I get, I just want to finish this course and get out of here!' is not uncommon, especially in a long course. If you are feeling low it is important to seek help so that you can again care about doing the best you can to fulfil your assessment tasks and study objectives. Caring is more beneficial than apathy.

MAINTAINING A GOOD DIET AND EXERCISE ROUTINE

Maintaining a healthy diet and exercise routine may seem like odd points in a book on academic study, but they are crucial to being effective as a student and in your other roles. A healthy diet will ensure you maintain the energy levels to sustain your workload. Often when things get a little hectic the first thing that slips is diet—but the consequences are soon apparent. Lots of caffeine or sugar-loaded snacks during high pressure times will only put you on a false high from which you will come crashing down. Take time out to eat well (think of the basic food groups) and have plenty of fresh vegetables, fruit and water. It is equally important to exercise regularly. This does not necessarily mean going to the gym or doing aerobics four times a week, especially if you really do not like such activities. Think of something you do enjoy—maybe walking or swimming. Take time out to do some form of exercise regularly during your week; and try not to let other commitments encroach on your exercise times. Your body and mind will thank you.

GETTING ORGANISED

Organisation is the key to reducing stress and maintaining effectiveness as a part-time student and in performing all your other roles. Try to get yourself organised as much as possible *before* your course begins—this will allow you to work effectively from the beginning. Of foremost importance is to set up a workable, private study space, that is respected by those around you, where you have your desk and all your notebooks, texts and so on. A double-usage space that needs to be cleared for other activities—the kitchen table, for instance—is far from ideal. Obtain the equipment you will need, such as stationery and computer equipment (see the study tools checklist provided at the end of this chapter), and organise an Internet connection if required. If your home does not allow you the luxury of a quiet space, investigate booking a student carrel for the semester or the year. Departments often set aside rooms for student use and some even come with computer equipment. Another retreat, though temporary, is the library, which will have private study rooms that you can book for a day or a number of days to work without being disturbed, which is very handy when you are working on an assignment.

The next step is to consider your preparedness. Many tertiary institutions offer a range of orientation courses that cover topics such as writing skills, general study skills, word processing, research skills, using the Internet and so on (usually run by the learning skills unit). Speak to someone in the Student Union for information on the details of such courses, which are normally free or offered to students at a reduced fee.

Before the course starts review the course outline to see what topics you will be covering, the assessment tasks required and the marks allotted; familiarise yourself with the timetable and check on required reading. From the outline or your initial discussions with your lecturer get an overall picture of what is expected of you. Skim read (see p. 73) the texts listed in the course outline or handbook if they are available beforehand; if not, find some other texts on the discipline to get a sense of the major issues. There is no need to be concerned about in-depth reading at this stage; instead, concentrate on getting a sense of the main arguments and how they interconnect.

TAKING RESPONSIBILITY AS A LEARNER

Tertiary students are expected to be self-reliant and self-directed ('self-directed learner' and 'independent learner' are common terms reflecting this fact). Self-directed learning does not mean that you need to teach yourself and not depend on your teachers apart from classes. Rather, it implies that you are responsible for developing the sorts of skills needed to undertake the course, which will mean becoming an organised, resourceful and critical thinker. Resourceful students will strive to locate the information, services or support facilities they need to ensure that their studies run smoothly. This might mean locating information in the library, seeking essay-writing assistance or making appointments to discuss learning issues with the lecturer. It involves being proactive in pinpointing what is required and taking the initiative in seeking appropriate information or assistance. In short, it means asking as many questions as required to get the answers.

IDENTIFYING YOUR SKILLS BASE

As a student you will use and fine-tune skills you already possess as well as develop new ones. Different disciplines place a different emphasis on certain skills. Appendix 2 outlines important general skills that will facilitate your learning. You might find it helpful to ascertain your skills level in terms of the eighteen different skills outlined in this list before the course begins, and again at the end of the first semester and the first year.

BECOMING A CRITICAL THINKER

A self-directed learner should be well on the way to developing critical thinking skills, but these are not developed overnight. Developing critical thinking is a process that will extend over the duration of your studies and beyond. It is the ability to select appropriate information, review, analyse and evaluate it. This analysis involves asking the six important inquiry questions: *Who? Why? What? When? Where? How?*

These six questions will facilitate your thinking about problem-solving activities. If you are unsure what a problem requires from you, try rewording it or breaking it into chunks, then reading it again as a whole. Think about where you can source information that will help you deal with the problem (will you need your class notes? extra reading?). By doing this you will be acting as a self-directed learner, making necessary links between information gathered.

Critical thinking is the ability to see the links between information and, importantly, to change information received to knowledge. As an independent critical thinker you will be responsible for making links between existing information and experience, and new information, to gain an understanding or knowledge base that brings you to a new level of knowledge. Remember that information remains *data* if not understood; once it is understood it can be absorbed to become *knowledge*.

To become a critical thinker you need to develop a detached attitude towards the information being analysed. This involves looking at the information from different perspectives (different sources/authors) and, while gaining an understanding of these other perspectives, being able to weigh up whether they are true or flawed. Critical thinking also means being able to build your own argument based on your analysis of these other perspectives, their truths or flaws, and your own ideas. Through your studies you will be able to practise and gain confidence in your ability to analyse information in this way. Some students pretend they are in a debate with a particular author and present arguments, evidence and questions for that author to respond to adequately. Others pretend to be investigative journalists who aim to investigate and analyse a piece of information.

If you feel you need feedback on your direction of inquiry,

make an appointment to see your lecturer, taking your notes and questions with you as a basis for discussion.

MINDMAPS

Some people prefer to work with a visual representation of their brainstorming or planning process, using mindmaps or concept maps. These come in as many styles as there are students. These visual representations can be drawn up as posters, pages or whiteboard sketches that are modified as the thinking process develops (an example appears in Figure 2.1). Even if you have not used it before, you might find this technique of assistance in developing your critical thinking on a subject.

Figure 2.1 Example of a mindmap

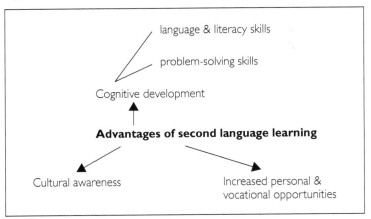

IDENTIFYING YOUR LEARNING STYLE

Everyone has a personal learning style. Your learning style generally dictates the aspects of your study environment that best elicit good learning and strong learning skills—in other words, it is how you prefer to learn. The checklist below, is based on the theory of multiple intelligences (Gardner, 1993) and can be used to identify patterns in your own learning style. (You can tick a range of responses in any one set of items.) The results should be used as a guide, rather than a comprehensive identification instrument, to the major patterns in your learning style. You will be able to use this information in thinking about yourself as a learner and a problem solver and in organising your study environment. Be wary of locking yourself into a 'type', however, as different tasks, pressures and moods are also factors in determining your study style at a particular time.

Having a sense of how you operate as a student will help you in creating the right sort of learning environment, being effective in your approach to learning and being patient with yourself when things seem a little tough. Becoming what can be termed a reflective learner is a step towards maintaining focus and motivation.

✓ CHECKLIST: UNDERSTANDING LEARNING STYLES

To remember new information, do you:

❑ Make a mental image of it?

❑ Set the information to music, e.g. make up rhymes or chants?

❑ Reread the information carefully, making sure you understand each word?

❑ Act out the information or follow it physically?

❑ Look carefully at the wording to work out such things as acronyms, jargon, use of vocabulary, etc.?

❑ Mull it over for a while?

❑ Discuss the information with someone?

When you are unsure of what words to use, or have difficulty explaining an idea, do you usually:

❑ Draw a picture to explain it?

❑ Refer to a piece of music or video clip to explain it?

❑ Draw a diagram?

❑ Act it out using mime or gesture?

❑ Use synonyms or other terms that mean the same thing, such as 'small portable phone' instead of 'mobile'?

❑ Spend more time thinking about the idea before having another try?

❑ Get help from someone?

What sort of relaxation activity do you prefer to break up your study?

❑ Doing an art or craft such as drawing, painting or going to a gallery.

❑ Listening to music.

❑ Designing things, working on calculations or computer programs.

❑ Playing sport.

❑ Doing crossword puzzles or other word games.

❑ Reading a book or doing something else on your own.

❑ Socialising with friends.

When you are preparing information for an assignment, do you:

❑ Brainstorm with lots of doodles, lines and other drawings, or perhaps watch videos on the subject?

❑ Use music to inspire you or contextualise the information, for instance, setting a scene in a book to a piece of music?

❑ Jot down ideas, then draw lines between them to demonstrate relationships?

❑ Enjoy the actual *doing* part of the assignment more than the *thinking* part of it, for instance, going to the library to look up information rather than sitting down to write?

❑ Think carefully about words and phrases that best represent the ideas you want to express before writing them down?

❑ Spend time on your own reflecting on the preparation process and information?

❑ Discuss ideas with others?

When you come across new information, do you:

❑ Try to visualise it so that you can remember it or 'absorb' it?

❑ Use music or chants to contextualise it or recall it?

❑ Look for patterns within it?

❑ Prefer to deal with it quickly and get on with the next bit?

❑ Repeat it over and over using your own words until you have memorised it?

❏ Try to make parallels with previous knowledge?

❏ Talk about it with others?

When you study, do you:

❏ Design a mindmap of what you are going to do?

❏ Have music playing in the background or hum along as you work?

❏ Plan what you are going to study each day?

❏ Work well for short bursts at a time?

❏ Think a lot about a subject before you start studying, particularly terms and phrases you will use or encounter?

❏ Prefer to work alone?

❏ Look for other people to form a study group or find a study partner?

When it comes to problem-solving situations, would you say you:

❏ Visualise the process or outcome, or spend time drawing or doodling as you think?

❏ Consider the problem while playing a musical instrument or with music in the background?

❏ Find out as much as you can about the problem, for instance, the reasons behind it, strategies for tackling it?

❏ Think about the problem while doing an activity, such as going for a walk or playing tennis?

❏ Look closely at the wording of the problem?

❑ Deal with it on your own by thinking about it for a while before trying to solve it?

❑ Deal with it in a group situation?

If you ticked mainly the first item in each set you tend to be a visual–spatial learner; second-item responses indicate a strong musical tendency; third-item responses indicate strong logical–mathematical tendencies; fourth-item responses demonstrate bodily–kinaesthetic inclinations. Fifth-item responses tend to demonstrate strong linguistic skills; sixth-item responses indicate intrapersonal (internal) inclinations to problem-solving, while the final item in each set indicates strong interpersonal tendencies in tackling learning situations. If you ticked a number of items in each set you probably have a varied range of learning styles and are quite flexible according to the situation. It is generally agreed that the most successful learners are those who can vary their learning style according to the situation.

There are positive aspects to each of these learning styles. However, you may find that other aspects of your style need developing to suit the demands of your scholarly role. Figure 2.3 lists learning styles and strategies, their positive aspects and areas that might need developing.

Figure 2.2 Learning styles and strategies

Learning style	Positive strategies	Aspects to develop
Visual–spatial	You have an ability for coordinating colours, form and other aspects of visual arts; you are good at:	You need to work on: • the ability to transfer your visual notes into written text or spoken communication

	• drawing or sketching ideas using mindmaps (or concept maps) • using your mindmap to see how new information links into previous knowledge and what this all means	
Musical	You have a strong awareness of rhythm and sound; you are good at: • using music to stimulate your thinking (music by Mozart and the Baroque composers is supposed to be very good 'thinking music'—if you are fond of classical music) • memorising or recalling information when it is set to music or chants	You need to work on: • the ability to work without external musical stimulus, particularly if you have written or oral exams
Logico-mathematical	You have an understanding of relationships between ideas or structures; you are good at: • designing mindmaps to	You need to work on: • the ability to spend time on details • the ability not to stress if information is missing, recognising

	organise information as you collect it • writing down questions as they spring to mind and using them as part of the problem-solving process • looking for patterns amongst your questions, the answers or the information you have collected	that you might just have to get on with the task as best you can under the circumstances
Bodily–kinaesthetic	You prefer activity to being sedentary and have well-developed fine and gross motor skills; you are good at: • hands-on activities • working in short bursts of activity rather than sitting for long periods • diving in to get things done without procrastinating • completing tasks	You need to work on: • the ability to spend a longer time at your desk, particularly if building up to exams • the ability not to be sidetracked from your thinking by doing something more active, for instance, organising your desk or computer rather than getting on with planning your essay
Linguistic	You are a good communicator (speaker/writer); you are good at:	You need to work on: • learning not to spend too much time on the details so that

	• working with letters, words and phrases • researching a problem through reading, taking note of any interesting language used • communicating ideas through speech or written text, or both	you leave enough time for completing the task
Intrapersonal	You do not find it difficult to spend time on your own; you are good at: • reflecting on yourself as a learner • listening skills • spending time on your own when trying to solve a problem • reflecting on a subject and the implications • time management skills • self-assessing of tasks	You need to work on: • learning to work in collaborative groups or partnerships • thinking too much about a subject or problem and eliminating any tendency to procrastinate • developing the ability to stick to your time management plan • developing the ability not to be so harsh on yourself and gaining more confidence
Interpersonal	You prefer the social side of learning to working on individual	You need to work on: • being more self-reliant as a learner

	tasks; you are good at: • communicating ideas to others • dealing with others, e.g. striking up a rapport with lecturers and fellow students • working collaboratively with others (e.g. study groups) • giving group presentations	• developing reflective skills that will assist you in dealing with problem-solving situations on your own • developing self-assessment skills so that you can assess your own work

ASSESSMENT

Assessment has an important role in tertiary studies. It gives both the lecturer and the student a record of progress—of the course objectives that have been fulfilled, and the areas of improvement—indicating the student's readiness to progress to the next level. Assessment records are also used in a professional context: applying for a job, to join a professional body, and so on.

Usually, assessment in higher education is not based on exams alone, but often on work submitted throughout the year plus exam results and class participation. In some courses which do not include exams, assessment is based mainly on assignments. Postgraduate research students, particularly at a Masters level, are assessed, in part or completely, on the research projects they submit. Assignments may include reports, essays, practicals, oral presentations, research projects, designs, pieces of artwork, or a mix of these. At the start of the course your lecturers will tell you what is expected from you and how many points are allocated to each task. You may also be provided with guidelines on how to set out your task; during the course the lecturer may also drop a few valuable hints. Regardless, ask the lecturer to explain if something is not clear.

Self-assessment is also useful in keeping you on track. The self-assessment checklist will help you think about your progress and ways to improve. Compare your answers with the comments made by your lecturers to gain an understanding of your strengths and the areas which need further improvement.

✓ CHECKLIST: SELF-ASSESSMENT

❑ What were my goals at the beginning of my studies?

❑ If my goals have changed, how have they changed?

❑ What are my strengths in my studies? (For instance, critical thinking, writing.)

❑ What are my weaknesses in my studies?

❑ What have I done to address my weaknesses? (For instance, reading every day, taking up conversation classes, doing an essay writing course.)

❑ What do I still have to do to address my weaknesses?

❑ Who do I feel comfortable talking to about study skills improvement?

GETTING ON WITH LECTURERS

The study process is often seen as a type of partnership in which the lecturer has the responsibility *to teach* by creating an appropriate learning environment, and the student has the responsibility of taking advantage of this environment *to learn*. Certain things will ensure that you maintain a good rapport with your lecturers. One is submitting assignments on time and presenting them well. Late and untidy documents do not smack of scholarly interest, and if you do not seem interested in the work, your lecturer might not be interested in you either. When you need to see your lecturer make an appointment as most of them are very busy with research and administrative commitments on top of their teaching load. (Remember also that some lecturers work on a sessional basis and will only be available at certain times.) On the whole, lecturers are very interested in you as a student and will invest time and energy in helping you with your studies. They do not want to see you fall behind. They were once students too, and they too have experienced life's ups and downs. If you do get behind, they will normally be able to help you get back on track, perhaps by organising extensions on assignment dates, setting make-up exams or providing lecture notes on missed classes. Do *not* wait until the last minute, however. Make time to speak to your lecturer *before* so much time gets away that you will be unable to catch up.

MAKING SOCIAL CONTACT

A common issue for part-time students is the sense of isolation that may result from having little contact with other students. With the number of constraints on their time, part-time students are usually found rushing—from one class to the next, from the library to the laboratory, from class to home. Fellow part-time students are often the greatest source of support, as they are probably experiencing the same problems with time constraints, work and family relationship pressures, and study issues. Forming a *study group* with other students in your class is a valuable way of getting both study and social support.

Educational institutions generally have a number of *clubs* and *associations* which provide a way of letting off steam and getting to know others. There are sporting clubs such as fencing, water polo and football, and associations such as chess, computer and religious societies. Even if you can attend only some of the meetings, you will still benefit from the social contact.

Studying is more than just being ready for the mechanics of reading and handing in assignments—you also need to be ready mentally, emotionally and academically. Spend some time thinking about yourself as a student and about the skills you need to implement. Consider the sort of environment you will have to create around yourself, then about your wider environment. Studying part time may impact upon a number of other aspects of your life, but if you are prepared you will be able to take up your new role as a student without losing a sense of balance.

✓ CHECKLIST: STUDY TOOLS

❑ A good one-day-to-a-page diary to jot down dates, tasks, important research items, thoughts and ideas to follow up, or to add to notes, etc.

❑ Weekly study schedule (see Chapter 3)

❑ Semester schedule (see Chapter 3)

❑ An A4 punched notebook for each subject or A4 lined punched paper, and an A4 ringed folder for each subject

❑ Books on the prescribed reading list

❑ Plastic envelopes for handouts and notes

❑ A good dictionary and thesaurus

❏   Pens, pencils, erasers, sharpeners, ruler(s), highlighters

❏   Computer (or arrange for computer access) with word processor, any other important packages, and printer

❏   Internet access if needed

❏   Computer disks

❏   Calculator

❏   Post-it$^{®}$ notes for note-taking

❏   Index cards for recording sources

❏   Lab coat if needed

3

Organising your study time

The key to successful part-time study is organising your time. Most part-time students are already juggling all sorts of activities, thus making a commitment to study often requires you to raise your organisational skills to another level. And it takes a little time to get things organised. It is worth considering the aspect of time management very carefully and planning your activities to ensure things go as smoothly as possible. Time management is particularly important to the part-time research student—at first glance it may seem that there is plenty of time to devote to study during a semester, but it is time which can very quickly disappear if you are not careful. This chapter discusses a number of ways of getting yourself organised and taking the stress out of a life split between the part-time student and the full-time person.

WEEKLY SCHEDULE

The first step in getting organised is to review your week. There is undoubtedly some element of routine in your weekly activities that will help you draft a schedule. Look at the overall picture, work out a daily timetable and stick to it as much as possible. Life has a way of throwing the unexpected at you, so allow yourself to be flexible and don't stress if you have to make sudden changes. A realistic, functional schedule will help you stay on track, lessen the opportunities for procrastination and keep you focused.

When you are drawing up the schedule, make sure you include *everything*—work hours and travel time, lectures and tutorials, any regular meetings, sports activities, religious observances. The next step is to work out realistically how much study time you will need each week to keep up with reading and assignments. Remember here that everyone works at a different pace so ensure that you give yourself enough time to study. Try not to schedule study time late at night when your energy levels are low. You also need enough sleep to cope with the next day's activities. There is a blank schedule in Appendix 8 to help you with drafting your own. Figure 3.1 is a weekly study schedule for a student who travels to work by train and prefers to do some reading while commuting each morning. She has Friday afternoons off to attend classes. As a mother of three young children she is also concerned that she devotes time to them and her husband.

After you have completed your own weekly schedule, and a study schedule for the semester (discussed in the next section), look carefully at the balance between your activities. There may be too much time devoted to study and not enough to your pastime, or vice versa. Do not fill in every space—it is important to leave some free time, real *free time* in which you can do nothing if you want to, or which you can use to catch up on things if it becomes necessary. Free time is valuable in keeping a sense of control and balance during your week; it is very easy to end up feeling as if the only things you do are study, work and be there for others.

Figure 3.1 Weekly schedule

Time	Monday	Tuesday	Wednesday	Thursday	Friday	Saturday	Sunday
8.00–8.45	Reading/travel	Reading/travel	Reading/travel	Reading/travel	Reading/travel	7.30–11am Reading & assignment preparation	Reading and note-taking
9.00–5.30	Work	Work	Work	Work	Work	11am Gym / 1pm Lunch / Family/free time	Lunch
					3pm Tutorial: Economics		
					4pm Assignment work (Library)	4–5.30 Reading	Social activities
5.30–6.15	Gym		5pm Gym	Dinner			
6.30–7.30	Dinner	Lecture: Finance	Dinner	Tutorial: Finance	Dinner		
7.30–8.30	Family time	Study Group: Finance	Family time	Lecture: Economics	Free time		
8.30–9.00	Review class notes. Tutorial tasks	Travel home	Research	Study Group (until 9.30 pm)	Free time	Evening social activities	Preparation and planning for coming week
9.00–10.00	Study	Family time	Assignment preparation	Travel home/ free time	Free time		

SEMESTER STUDY SCHEDULE

A semester study schedule is a little trickier as it means gauging how much time will be taken up preparing assignments, but it is worth the effort. It gives you the opportunity to plan around activities such as holiday breaks, conferences and social activities. Figure 3.2 is the semester schedule of the student whose weekly schedule appears in Figure 3.1 Appendix 8 includes a blank semester study schedule to help you draft your own.

Figure 3.2 Semester study schedule

Semester Weeks	Economics	Finance
1	Planning and literature search Take notes	Planning and literature search for essay
2	Complete tutorial assignment	Note-taking for essay Complete first draft
3	Holiday break	Holiday break
4	Redraft and submit **Tutorial Assignment due**	Complete second draft and check references
5	Literature search. Notes. Tutorial assignment	Edit and submit. **Essay due** Revise Topics 1–3
6	Complete Sections A & B Tutorial assignment	Revise Topics 4–6
7	Complete Section C Redraft tutorial assignment	Practice Exams

8	Submit (Weekend away) **Tutorial Assignment due**	Weekend away
9	Literature search Tutorial assignment	Planning of oral presentation with group Literature search
10	Complete Sections A & B Tutorial assignment	Initial reading and note-taking Second meeting with group to organise points
11	Complete Section C Redraft assignment	Oral Presentation— practise **Oral Presentation due**
12	**Tutorial Assignment due**	Practice Exams and Revision
13	**End of semester**	**Exam**

AVOIDING TIME-WASTING TRAPS

Cramming your schedule

Listing the tasks to be done each day of the week in a diary is a quick and effective way of getting organised, particularly during stressful periods. Prioritise each task, and as each one is done, physically tick it off your list. By the end of the day, or the week, you will have achieved all or most of what you intended to, and things will look a lot clearer. If you have not achieved enough, perhaps your list is too long and you need to work out what needs to be done by *you*. Perhaps someone else in the house can take over some of the chores for a while. Perhaps you can delegate tasks at work so that you are not bringing work home.

Always late?

There is nothing more stressful than lack of time. A lot of unnecessary energy is wasted fretting over being late for a class or an appointment with a lecturer. The key is to be organised to leave 15 minutes *ahead* of schedule. This may mean downing tools dead on time, cutting short a conversation with a colleague, postponing a phone call and leaving work or home to get to classes with a few minutes to spare. Often the most important minutes of the study day are those 15 minutes when you leave home/work behind and start thinking about the class topic or go over the points you wanted to raise with your lecturer.

Procrastinating

Avoid procrastination by keeping an eye on your schedule and the progress of your task. Anxiety over an essay can keep you from putting pen to paper and make you feel that you are doing something equally worthwhile by reading more than you need to. Eventually there comes a time when you have to put the book down and start writing. Using a word processor can help. You can just start writing, putting down anything you can think of that's relevant, even in a jumbled fashion. When you have those immediate thoughts down, print out what you've got and start planning. Chapter 6 on writing has suggestions to guide you.

Taking time off

Another pitfall is cramming your schedule with too many activities. If you have had a busy day at work, try not to cram in yet another taxing meeting. Pace yourself over the week and reschedule that meeting for a slower day. Give yourself time to get things done and leave a little energy for yourself at the end of the day. On those inevitable days when everything needs to be done by yesterday, take time out to take a deep breath and prioritise tasks. Work out what can be delegated or postponed. Whenever it all gets too much, take a five-minute relaxation break and start again. If your life seems too full of these crazy days maybe you need to look at how to shed some of your taskload.

When something comes up that interferes with your study schedule, don't stress about it. If you have the chance to get away for a weekend, go without feeling guilty—forget your studies and make it a real break. A spontaneous weekend off or an evening out at a concert are good ways to recharge the batteries so that you feel ready to study again.

Recording sources

Keeping a comprehensive record of your course and assignment reading goes a long way towards saving valuable time at the end. Although the bibliography or references list is generally dealt with at the end of an assignment, always note down each reference you use as you read it during the drafting process. Writing down bibliographical details (see Chapter 5) on bits of paper instead of on a proper working document means you risk losing them and having to search them out again.

'I'm on the Net'

The Internet, while it can be a valuable research tool, can also be a real time waster. You may feel as if you are studying but you may just as easily be procrastinating or wasting time. A lot of time can be wasted surfing, following endless links and going down irrelevant tracks. Keep your research direction focused and know when to stop surfing and get on with studying. Chapter 12 looks at effective techniques for using electronic sources for research.

Using e-mail

Be ruthless with your e-mails. Reply, file or delete rather than leaving them sitting on your machine. One strategy is to check your e-mail at the end of the day rather than in the morning when you should be getting going. If you can't leave it to the end of the day, allocate a specific time for reading e-mail and don't be tempted into being sidetracked by unimportant messages. The first thing to do when you open up is to ignore and delete all junk mail.

MAINTAINING MOMENTUM

Taking breaks is one of the best ways of recharging your energy levels. Students who work frenetically, stressing out because they are late with their assignments, often find that their energy levels dip drastically. They end up going around in circles with what they are trying to think or write. It is important to take regular breaks—for some people this is five minutes every hour, for others five minutes every two hours. At home, resist the temptation to make that quick phone call to your friend; you may end up talking for much longer than five minutes. Get a glass of water instead or have a quick walk around the garden. In the library, stretch your legs with a short walk or get a drink.

Reward yourself for getting things done on time and being productive by doing something you really like. One student who was undertaking research studies would treat herself to an afternoon at an art gallery—but only if she had finished the work she had planned for the week.

PROTECT YOUR STUDY TIME

Protecting your study time is a hard lesson to learn, but learn it early and things will run more smoothly on the whole. Remember how important it is that your partner, family, friends and colleagues understand how much your studies mean to you. Study does not just happen when they are not around. When you have your schedule organised let them know when you will *not* be available. Then go to your study space, close the door and ignore all non-emergency phone calls and taps on the door. Turn on your answering machine and put up a sign on the door saying 'Please do not disturb' or 'I will be available at 3pm'.

PROTECT YOUR FREE TIME

Your free time is just as important as your study time. Make the most of it, switch off and allow yourself to enjoy the feel of the wind in your hair as you go for a jog, playing with your children, the company of your partner over dinner or a movie you have been dying to see. There is no reason to feel guilty about that half-written essay on your desk. Enjoy the moment and go back to your essay feeling refreshed.

Some people find that their social life diminishes during the course of their studies and they feel alienated from their friends. Keeping up your friendships is important, but at times you will need to make a special effort. Perhaps lessen the time involved by having informal takeaway dinners or a quick cup of coffee to keep in touch.

TIME MANAGEMENT FOR THE RESEARCH STUDENT

As a research student you are in charge of using your time effectively. Again, a weekly schedule and a semester study schedule will help. As part of your research proposal you will need to submit a timeline that demonstrates a longitudinal view of your activities over the whole course. It is vital that all three schedules are realistic and workable. Use your appointments with your supervisor to keep yourself on track. Ensure you have something down on paper each time you meet—any questions regarding the reading or methodology, or some drafted material. Organise a set of appointments throughout the year so that time is not lost in chasing each other up.

Time management is an aspect of study which needs constant review. Your weekly and semester study schedules will assist you in getting into a routine and avoiding time-wasting traps. They will also ensure that along with reading, your assignments and other tasks are spread out over the study period rather than left to the last minute (which means less stress and a more rewarding study experience).

4

> **There can be no fairer ambition than to excel in talk.**
>
> Robert Louis Stevenson

Participating in classes

The notion of entering into academic argument refers to the process of reasoning to come to solid conclusions. Reasoning is demonstrated through a number of aspects of a course, such as written work, class discussions, oral presentations and assignments. It is important to take advantage of the opportunities given in class to extend your knowledge. In practical terms, your participation in class may also be counted towards your assessment score.

CLASS TYPES

Several types of classes may be scheduled for your course, depending on the subject: lectures, tutorials, workshops, seminars and lab sessions.

Lectures are generally held for all the participants in a course or for groups ranging from 30 to 300 students. The bigger they are the less opportunity there is to interact with the lecturer by asking questions; thus lectures become a time for you to gain an overview of the topic and take notes. A lecture might be an hour long or extend for several hours, and might be held once or repeated a number of times a week, depending on the course. Prepare for each lecture by doing the recommended reading. It pays to get to a lecture early so that you are assured of a seat, have time to get your notes ready and are present when handouts are distributed. While it is sometimes difficult to concentrate for a lengthy period in such an artificial environment it is important that you learn to do so, as lectures provide a useful overview of the topic that will assist your reading and often guide your line of critical thinking. The lecturer may also drop hints about assessment tasks or exams, so be aware. Try not to fall into the trap of note-taking for its own sake but take clear succinct notes outlining the topic that will assist your later work. Note-taking should not detract from the primary reason you are there—to listen. Resist the temptation to skip lectures and rely on the lecture notes published on websites, which are normally abbreviated. It is always better to attend lectures in person unless the web-based lectures have been especially designed to cater to the needs of distance students.

The topic introduced in the lecture is covered in more detail in smaller classes or **tutorials**, and through your reading. Smaller classes offer the opportunity for you to participate actively—here you can bring up issues, ask questions, clarify confusing points, get feedback and explore ideas in more detail. Doing your reading and any tutorial/workshop tasks ahead of time will enable you to better utilise the time spent in these classes.

Seminars are held when someone is invited to talk on a particular topic—a staff member, someone outside the university, sometimes another student. The topic is presented and for the rest of the time the seminar concentrates on discussing various aspects of the topic. If you are required to present as part of a seminar series, the section on giving a presentation (p. 54) details how to prepare and present an oral presentation, both individually and as part of a group.

Laboratory (lab) or **practical sessions** allow students to practise technical skills under the supervision of the lecturer. They are common in science and engineering courses.

Study groups may be formed by a lecturer or by students themselves and provide an ideal opportunity for exchanging ideas, getting a different perspective on a topic, sharing experiences, getting assistance and practising argument. Lecturers may arrange study groups to undertake group assignments; however, you might organise one to give added opportunities to go over tutorial tasks, reading or assignments. They help otherwise isolated part-time students to feel part of the academic community, and often serve to keep you on track with your study plans. Study groups may take some effort to get established but are worth it. Meeting regularly just before or after class over a snack and a coffee is a good way of keeping up their momentum.

CRITICAL LISTENING SKILLS

One of the most important skills you will use in class participation is critical listening, also termed 'passive participation'. At times it will seem that you have been bombarded with so much information in a class that your head is spinning. This in itself is an exciting part of learning, but by developing critical listening skills you will be able to utilise the time spent in class more effectively. Listen carefully to the speaker, and decipher the information or argument being presented in terms of accuracy, hidden assumptions, *reason*ableness and logic. The questions in the checklist of critical listening skills will guide you in developing these skills, which will help your note-taking as well as your ability to argue confidently in class.

✓ **CHECKLIST: DEVELOPING CRITICAL LISTENING SKILLS**

❑ What is the speaker's main argument?

❑ What evidence is given?

❑ How does the speaker's argument correlate with what you know from other class discussions or reading you have done?

❑ Are there any hidden assumptions?

❑ Are there any hidden agendas?

❑ How does the speaker's argument correlate with your own perspective on the topic?

❑ How can you challenge the speaker's argument?

GIVING AN ORAL PRESENTATION

The prospect of giving an oral presentation in front of your peers and lecturers can be daunting, but with proper preparation and an understanding of the process you will be less nervous and the results will be positive. The idea of a presentation is to communicate your ideas by developing an argument delivered in a way that is interesting to a live audience rather than to a reader. It is a valuable way of getting immediate feedback through the comments and questions raised at the end of the presentation. This section outlines the steps involved in preparing a general presentation, an oral report and a group presentation, and covers such aspects as maintaining eye contact, preparing visuals and capturing the attention of the audience. Your lecturer will assess both content and delivery, using criteria similar to those outlined in Appendix 2. Familiarity with a lecturer's criteria for assessment can be helpful.

STRUCTURING A PRESENTATION

A presentation is similar to an essay in that it must include an introduction, a main body and a conclusion. There is usually time set aside afterwards for questions from the audience.

The **introduction** gives you the opportunity to outline what you are going to talk about and the steps you are going to take in presenting the talk. Here you might give some background information on the issue or 'set the scene' by mentioning its importance, and also set the tone of the talk. If you want to present a talk that does not have a strong formal tone, you might drop in a joke or anecdote. This will not make your talk less interesting or important; instead, it often serves to make your point more clearly without depending on the traditional conventions of formal speaking. The beginning of the talk provides the ideal opportunity to capture the audience's attention. The first impression is important, so make your introduction clear and strong.

Students who are not comfortable with the humorous approach might focus the audience on their talk and set the tone by using a catchy phrase or quote or asking a question. Another good focusing technique is to use a cartoon or other appropriate visual aid (remember, a picture can speak a thousand words). You can put these up on an overhead projector. Once you have engaged the interest of your audience you are ready to go. Do not worry too much about making a traditional presentation—sometimes a different strategy is a welcome relief from the same old stuff and it certainly gives the audience (including the lecturer) something to think about.

The **main argument** constitutes the body of the presentation. This is where you present each main point and its relevant supporting issues, identify any contradictions you have found and mention interesting readings, points or findings. In this section include the important issues relating to the argument and explanations of their relevance. Use linking phrases or 'connectives' (see p. 91) to demonstrate links between ideas so that the audience remains focused on your topic. (Try not to always use the same few linking words.) You need to include your evidence or results for each of the issues presented, just as you would in a report or essay, so you will need to draw on other sources.

The **conclusion** is the final part of the presentation and it is just as important as the rest of it. Many students undermine their hard work by finishing with 'That's it' or a simple summary. While it is important to return to the question and summarise the key elements raised in the body of your presentation, it is just as important to leave your audience with something to think about regarding the topic. You can make an impact in your summary using the same sorts of strategies as in the introduction (perhaps a question, a picture or quote).

Figure 4.1 Techniques for capturing audience attention

a cartoon	a quote
a catchy phrase	a question
a short video	a joke
a few interesting statistics	a piece of music
an anecdote	an audience-participation activity
a picture	related to the topic

Handling question time

Question time is usually the last stage of the presentation and it should not be a cause for nervousness. It is a chance for the audience to ask you questions about aspects of the topic or share their reflections or experiences. Listen carefully to each question. The sense of relief that the presentation is practically over often leads to the importance of this component being overlooked, but it is one of the most valuable and interesting parts of your presentation. It provides an ideal opportunity to give further explanations of various points, to get a sense of the degree of interest your topic raises, and may highlight areas that need to be worked on or emphasised more strongly. Such feedback through question time is particularly valuable for ongoing research work. If the questions involve more detailed responses than your preparation allows, it is acceptable to explain that further research into that aspect will be needed before you can give an appropriate answer. You do not have to have the answers to every possible question on the subject. If you are unsure, say so. You can offer to investigate the matter further, explain that the particular information required is not really related to the focus of your topic, or suggest that it would make an interesting topic in itself. Listening to other speakers handling question times may suggest other strategies you could adopt. Maintain eye contact during question time, just as you did throughout the presentation, so that everyone feels included, not just the person who asked the question (see p. 60–61).

Figure 4.2 summarises the steps in preparing a general presentation.

Figure 4.2 Preparing a general presentation

Outline:
- title of topic
- name of presenter(s)
- course name
- date presented

Introduction:
- define the topic and its relevance to the course, etc.
- state the main ideas you will be presenting
- explain the steps you will be taking during the presentation

Issue one:
- present the issue
- outline supporting arguments or evidence

Issue two:
- present the issue
- outline supporting arguments or evidence

Issue three:
- present the issue
- outline supporting arguments or evidence

Conclusion:
- summarise the key points of the argument
- make a strong statement about the argument that leaves the audience with something to think about

Question time

PRESENTING A REPORT OR RESEARCH PROJECT

Preparing an oral report on research or events is a little different to giving a general presentation. While the aims of the **introduction** and **conclusion** are similar, the **body** of the presentation covers different aspects, including, firstly, the *background details* of the study: who was involved in carrying out the research; the relevance of the topic and any other necessary information. Next you should outline the *methodology* used, including such aspects as: subject background; important details on what was being studied; where and how the information was obtained; the timeline involved and so on. The *findings* make up the third section, in which the interesting and important aspects of your study findings are presented to the audience. When a report throws up other questions that might need investigating, the next section, **recommendations,** provides an opportunity to outline suggestions for areas needing further research. This section also gives you a chance to demonstrate your critical thinking skills by analysing the topic within a broad context. Here you may also present thoughts on alternative steps or means of conducting research on the topic. You might also use this section to mention any problems that occurred in gathering your information and explain how you resolved them, if this was possible, or would resolve them in another situation. Unresolvable problems do not mean that the study you undertook was not correct; recognising them shows that you have reflected sufficiently on the whole process to enable you to offer constructive alternatives or improvements. You then move on to the **conclusion**, following the principles outlined on p. 60.

Figure 4.3 summarises these steps to assist your planning.

Figure 4.3 Presenting a report or research project

Introduce the following details (a slide, overhead or handout with the following details is often effective):

* title of the topic
* name of presenter(s)
* course name
* date presented

Introduction:

* define the topic
* list the main points of the argument

Background to the topic:

* detail who was involved
* explain why the topic has been chosen, its relevance to the course and/or importance to the discipline or society in general

Methodology:

* explain the steps in undertaking your research
* outline timeline or schedule of the project

Findings:

* describe what you found out about the topic

Recommendations:
- offer suggestions for areas needing further research
- outline any problems encountered and how you resolved them (if possible)

Conclusion:
- outline an overview of key points
- finish with a strong statement regarding your topic

Question time

MAKING YOUR TALK INTERESTING

Selecting your own topic

Your lecturer may give you the opportunity to select a topic in which you are really interested. This is a good opportunity to present a talk on something you feel strongly about or would like to explore in more depth. Certainly, it is much easier to research and present a lively talk on something that interests you than on something you do not understand fully or find boring.

Talk to the topic and maintain eye contact

Talk to the topic. It is very easy to lose time and marks by bringing in interesting but irrelevant issues which only confuse the listener. Explain all the terms you use in the presentation—you should not assume that everyone is familiar with them. Speak in a natural voice, and try to be expressive (without being dramatic) by varying your intonation. Reading directly from your paper is not always the easy option. If you do prefer to read however, it pays to develop a reading style which highlights important and interesting points while sounding as natural as possible; if you read in a monotonous manner you will lose audience interest very quickly. Maintain eye contact with the whole audience (not just one side of the room) as this helps to keep your listeners engaged with your message. If you find eye contact difficult, try focusing at a level just above your listeners' heads. Eye contact sends out a message of honesty, knowledge and confidence. If you are looking down at your papers, chances are that the audience will be looking down at their papers too!

Preparing visuals

Overheads or slides, if they are appropriate to your topic, work well as prompting notes for yourself and as a tool to keep your listeners focused on the main points of the presentation. Keep overheads neat and do not crowd them with too much information; sometimes a simple picture is more effective than a page of words. Choose an appropriate type size; the most inspiring visuals are useless if they cannot be seen from the back of the room. Keep slides few in number as well—having a lot may mean the audience is so busy taking them all in that they have no time to listen to your talk.

Computer programs such as PowerPoint allow you to create some very effective slides with pictures, graphs and video. If it is not feasible to present the slides using a computer and projector, they can be printed out and photocopied onto overhead transparencies (OHTs). In fact, even if you have a computer-based slide presentation and all the technical equipment is prepared, prepare your visuals as OHTs as well, just in case there is a technical hitch.

It's a question of practise

Rehearse your presentation until you feel comfortable with the content and have memorised your key points. This will help reduce nerves and keep you focused. Keep to the time limit as you rehearse, and leave time at the end for questions. You might allot a time for each section so that on the day you neither rush nor run out of time. Consider tone and pace. Practise aloud, speaking as you would during your presentation—this will help you work out the right sort of tone for the talk. Speaking aloud helps you get used to hearing the sound of your own voice, which is particularly important if you are not used to giving presentations. Remember an important point is highlighted by a pause, a slower pace and a slightly raised voice. Some students find it helpful to rehearse using a tape recorder, adjusting their speaking patterns in response to the playback.

Another way of facilitating the communication process is through body language, though the degree to which people use it varies widely. Many English speakers tend to slow their speech, pause and look their audience in the eye when emphasising a point, which helps create an air of shared intimacy. Due to cultural or personal traits, however, many other people find it difficult to maintain this style of eye contact. You will have to think of strategies that you are comfortable with. Observing the body language that other people (your lecturers?) use will help—at the very least it might help you sort out good strategies from bad!

COPING WITH NERVES

It is perfectly natural to be nervous about standing up in front of your peers, particularly if you are being assessed. You might find that you are nervous even if you are generally confident or are used to giving presentations as part of your job. It is no secret that the key to controlling nervousness is preparation and confidence in what you are presenting. As a teacher once told me, if you are not nervous then something is not right. A degree of nervousness will stimulate you to try your best rather than being complacent. Strategies to contain an attack of 'presentation nerves' include:

- Deep breathing exercises beforehand or try the relaxation technique (p. 20–21).
- Smile to yourself (and the audience) before you start.
- As you move from one slide to the next, take two or three deep breaths.
- Maintain an even speaking voice throughout; this will help you feel more confident and certainly ensures a more polished presentation.
- Take a drink of water as you move from one slide to the next; this gives you time to take a deep breath and keep a positive focus.
- If maintaining eye contact makes you feel even more nervous, try looking just above everyone's heads.
- Recruiting an encouraging friend to sit in the audience can help.
- If you are prone to fidget when nervous, hold your hands lightly together in front of you.
- Nervous body gestures such as snorting, sniffing or twisting your fingers tend to distract your audience, so try to control them.
- Act as if you have no doubts about the value of your presentation; this helps you deliver with confidence.
- Remember that everyone wants you to do well and wants to hear and see your presentation—so don't worry!

SELF-ASSESSMENT

Immediately after the presentation, take a little time to relax and enjoy the feeling of accomplishment. In the next day or so, however, take some time to go over the presentation content and your performance. Such self-assessment will put you in a position to improve your next presentation. Another useful activity is to compare your reflections with the feedback provided by your lecturer.

PREPARING A GROUP PRESENTATION

The steps involved in preparing a presentation as a group are a little different to planning one individually. The keys to success are to ensure everyone has input into its organisation, does an equal amount of work and feels able to discuss issues with the rest of the group. There must also be opportunities to practise the presentation as a group. Figure 4.4 gives a step-by-step guide.

Figure 4.4 Steps in preparing a group presentation

First meeting:
1. Meet to discuss the topic and brainstorm the issues which will become the main and supporting ideas.
2. Group the points as main and supporting points (you might use headings).
3. Roughly allocate how much time should be devoted to presenting each issue.
4. Allocate research and writing-up tasks amongst the members of the group to be done before the next meeting.
5. Draft your handouts.
6. Draft your slides.

Second meeting:
1. Review the main issues to be presented, making sure everything is included.
2. Go over your supporting arguments and evidence.
3. Ensure the introduction and conclusion are clear and effective.
4. Make sure there are links between each other's sections, for example:
   As my colleague has explained . . .
   As has been demonstrated . . .
   As the next speaker will outline . . .
5. Redraft overheads and handouts.
6. Brainstorm possible questions that may be asked and jot down notes for answers.
7. Practise the presentation as a group, more than once to get it right.

When working in a group it is important to establish ground rules that will ensure everyone feels valued and confident about contributing. Simple courtesy, such as listening to everyone, can ensure that each person's ideas can be built on and that one member does not dominate the group. Disagreements handled in a constructive way, and admitting mistakes, can also be key ingredients in productive group work. Sharing ideas and the workload ensures that everyone feels included.

Utilising class time through active discussion and questioning is a valuable way of forming thoughts, getting feedback, clarifying understandings and gaining other perspectives on an issue. Presenting formally is an extension of this process and should be viewed as a way of collaborating through the sharing of information, not a 'test of character'.

✓ CHECKLIST: ORAL PRESENTATIONS

❑ Is the introduction concise and effective?

❑ Are the main points identifiable?

❑ Does each main point have supporting evidence?

❑ Are the issues raised in a logical order?

❑ Have you defined all the terms used?

❑ Do the ideas flow? Have you used appropriate signalling phrases?

❑ Does the conclusion provide an overview of the main ideas?

❑ Does the conclusion make an impact?

❑ Are all the notes and visuals in order?

❑ Are there too many visuals?

❑ Are the visuals relevant?

❑ Are the visuals presented clearly?

❑ Are the handouts complete?

❑ Have you rehearsed the presentation so that you feel comfortable with it?

❑ Have you thought about possible questions that may be asked during question time? How about possible answers to questions?

❑ Is the timing of the presentation realistic?

❑ Have you worked on delivering the presentation in an even tone (not monotone)?

Now just be confident—your positive attitude will influence the audience as well!

> **Polonius: What do you read, my lord?**
> **Hamlet: Words, words, words.**
>
> Shakespeare, *Hamlet*

5

Reading and note-taking

A lot of time is spent reading and note-taking during a course. Both activities assist with memory and organising of thoughts but are often undervalued in the study process. Good note-taking and reading skills can assist in formulating and articulating ideas. A lot of time can be wasted here, but with practise you will develop time-saving strategies to deal with these elements. This chapter looks at such things as choosing reading material, becoming a critical reader and developing varied reading and note-taking techniques to deal with different situations.

When your course starts you need to be diligent about reading and note-taking, not to the point of being so focused on your studies alone that you burn out in one semester, but so that you get into an efficient study routine. This will save you a lot of stress and facilitate assignment and exam preparation.

REASONS FOR READING

Reading will be one of your major study activities. You will find yourself reading different types of documents, both print and electronic based, for different purposes. It may seem a trivial point, but it is important to recognise the purpose for which you are reading so that you can adopt an appropriate reading strategy and note-taking process to allow you to read effectively. You may need to read to:

- prepare for an assignment;
- prepare for classes;
- get a sense of the arguments, both contradictory and similar;
- expand your knowledge of points covered in class; or
- prepare for an exam.

CHOOSING APPROPRIATE READING MATERIAL QUICKLY

You might start your reading with the texts from the recommended reading lists in the course handbook or the subject outlines. The references listed in these texts will lead to other relevant information. If you have few leads you might start a general library or online search. In this case it can happen that you start reading in the hope of stumbling across a rich vein of information but instead find yourself frustrated and lost in a mountain of confusing material. To avoid wasting time and effort you need to develop strategies for pinpointing appropriate material quickly, which means you need to know how print-based and electronic materials work. It may sound obvious, but the first thing to do is to run your eye over the material to gauge its relevance. The criteria listed in Figure 5.1 will help with this important process; they apply to both paper and web-based material.

Figure 5.1 Criteria for initial evaluation of reading material

- The title: Does it seem relevant?
- The author: What is the writer's experience? Is the person(s) unknown or seen as an authority?
- The date of publication: Is the book outdated?
- Publisher (if applicable): Where is it published? Overseas material might be more relevant to the general international scene.
- The contents page (if applicable): Does it appear to cover issues in which you are interested?
- The blurb on the back cover and the introduction: Does the information here seem relevant to your reading purpose?
- References: Are these recognisable? Are they comprehensive, indicating that the text has been well researched? (Once you begin reading on a topic you will see the same authoritative names appearing in much of the material you select, giving an indication of whether the source has been well researched or not.)
- The text itself: From a quick scanning, is it written in a comprehensible style? (You are much more likely to carry out a reading task well when you are not put off by extraordinarily formal or jargon-packed text. You might not have a choice in the matter of reading material but if you do, find material that is easily understood and suits your purposes.)
- Is there any bias? For instance, does a particular company have a commercial interest in the line of argument presented? If this is the case, consider the value of the text to your argument.

USING THE LIBRARY

Most libraries have a number of different desks where you can get assistance. The main desk is where you usually borrow books or equipment, the information desk is where you go with queries about accessing or locating library resources, and the reserve desk holds materials that subject lecturers have put on restricted access.

Modern computerised catalogue and library service systems enable a lot of the legwork to be done from your computer at home (or at work if this is permitted). You can gain access to your institution's library through the Internet and search for materials. Your search can be extended to other libraries around the world that have put their catalogues online. You can undertake literature searches online as well. These are usually discipline-based. Chapter 12 explores online searching in more detail.

Postgraduate students will have access to interlibrary loans, which means you can request materials such as journal articles, conference proceedings and texts from other institutions if your own does not have them. As the process can take several weeks it is best to be organised well in advance of any assignment or chapter submission dates.

The library reference section houses general texts such as dictionaries, thesauri, encyclopaedias, maps, atlases and manuals which are not available for loan.

The journals or periodicals for various disciplines, which provide an effective way of keeping up to date with the latest discussions and research, are kept in a separate section of the library and normally cannot be borrowed. Not all libraries house all journals but you can access articles from journals located at other institutions through the interlibrary loan process. Some journals are now available online through libraries. Local, interstate and overseas newspapers are also available. Check with the subject librarian or your lecturer regarding those specific to your discipline.

Due to space limitations, many libraries make use of microfiche and microfilm, most often for old newspapers, government documents and periodicals. The film can be read on special readers that magnify the text.

Most libraries have a number of photocopiers which you can use. Note that photocopies are permitted for personal use only and copyright regulations apply.

The audio-visual section normally contains tapes, CDs and videos and equipment such as overhead projectors, video players and digital cameras that can be borrowed for a limited period. It pays to check that they are working before borrowing them.

Most libraries contain some computers for student use, though more are found in student laboratories. They generally have Internet access and a word-processing package on them, but not a wide range of other programs. It pays to investigate whether the program you need is available in the library, as a student computer lab may be a better option.

BECOMING A CRITICAL READER

To avoid the frustration and inefficiency of reading a lot of useless material, or reading without understanding, it is important to become a critical reader. This means treating the reading process as an active rather than passive activity, and adopting a critical, questioning attitude to the material you are reading. The term 'critical' is used in the sense of actively thinking about what you are reading as you are reading it, not in the sense of being negative. Look for the real message and its relevance for your purpose. Question the material, engage with it so that you can decide whether it is worth reading or worth discarding. Question the material so that you can get information from your reading of it that will help you with your studies. Consider the writer's argument; it may be inadequately supported or even unreasonable, in which case there may be cause for you to respond through critical argument. The questions in Figure 5.2 will help you in developing critical reading skills.

Figure 5.2 Developing critical reading skills

- What is the writer's purpose? Who is the material written for?
- Is the author a well-known specialist in the field?
- What arguments are presented? How are they supported? (You should look at the author's theoretical or philosophical stance to see what perspective has been taken.)
- Are there any assumptions or hidden agendas in the writer's purpose?
- How does the information correlate with what has been presented in the course so far?
- If there is no agreement between this reading and your course notes, reading or experiences, what are the contrary issues and what evidence is presented to support them?
- How does the material fit with your own thoughts and experiences?
- How does it fit with other reading you have done?
- Does the information seem valid in terms of the supporting arguments or evidence presented?
- Is the information relevant to your reading purpose?

EFFICIENT READING AND NOTE-TAKING

As you progress in your studies you will become more efficient as an active reader and note-taker. You will develop techniques that will suit your learning style and time constraints. A vital aspect of efficient reading and note-taking is to read with a purpose and to maintain this focus so that your notes are relevant. There are, of course, times when you will come across points that at first do not seem important but later turn out to be main issues. If you get a sense of an argument that may be relevant to the topic, jot down the source with page numbers and key words in your note-taking recording system (see pp. 79–82) so you can easily retrace it.

Take note that you are neither reading nor note-taking efficiently if you are copying down large slabs of material, particularly if none of your own comments on the material appear in the margin alongside.

SELECTING A READING TECHNIQUE

Reading for academic purposes means that you have to get through a lot of material rather quickly. While you cannot be expected to read everything in depth, you will be expected to have a good grasp of the main ideas, which means that you need to develop skills in changing the pace and method of how you read. It is particularly important to be able to get through a large amount of material quickly when dealing with web-based material. The use of hypertext (which allows you to move from one bit of information to another by clicking on links) means that reading is broken into non-sequential chunks. Thus, you need to rely on memory, critical thinking and note-taking skills even more, perhaps, than when dealing with paper-based information.

One technique to assist you in reading quickly is **skim reading**. Skim reading (and scanning) involves running your eye over a text quickly to pick up the main ideas; some people run their finger across the page to guide them as they skim. To skim read effectively you must be an active reader attuned to picking up key words and phrases. Reading parts of the text will also allow you to grasp a sense of the argument without spending too much time poring over the text—this is a very helpful skill when you have a lot of reading to do and limited time. Examining the abstract, the introduction, the first line of each paragraph, then skimming over the text and reading the conclusion are the basics of the skim-reading process.

Scanning is similar to skimming in terms of being a quick reading technique, but involves a more purposeful attitude; you scan a text looking for specific information. For instance, if you are reading to answer a particular question, you will scan a text for the key words, phrases or graphic information that will show you the text is relevant to your purpose, rather than to get the gist of an argument. Scanning will save a lot of time and effort in selecting the parts of a text, if any, on which you should concentrate. However, it must be done purposefully, reading actively, or you will find that you are not taking in the sense of the material.

In-depth reading, on the other hand, involves taking the time to digest all the aspects of the text that would be missed by skimming or scanning. You might be reading to get a comprehensive sense of the text's main and supporting ideas and the relationship between them, to analyse the writer's methods or style, or to investigate the logic of the arguments presented. In-depth reading involves a process of questioning or critically analysing the text or its arguments, or both. This may involve taking time to both read the information for specific issues and to step back to see how the whole text works in terms of presenting the argument.

Learning to switch to the technique appropriate to a task will take a little time and experience but is an important part of learning to be a student, given the amount of reading you will have to do and the deluge of information that generally comes up in online searches. You may find yourself switching between the three techniques in the one document. As you master critical reading techniques you will find that you will become the best judge of the technique required, and become attuned to taking a questioning attitude.

REASONS FOR NOTE-TAKING

Before we launch into note-taking strategies, consider the purpose behind your note-taking. The purpose will guide the type of recording that you undertake. Note-taking allows you to record important details and to remember important issues—it means jotting down key words, short phrases, questions and important points to jog your memory, *not* simply copying down slabs of information. Notes can be used for general understanding of an issue, as a memory aid and in the preparation of assignments and exams. They are helpful tools in recording your own ideas and juxtaposing them against the ideas presented in a text or in classes, thus assisting the process of critical thinking. If the assessment requirements of your course include exams, the note-taking you do during your studies will stand you in good stead for exam preparation.

Rereading your notes at the end of every week or two, and as you finish each topic, will ensure that you are constantly refreshing your thoughts about the issues raised in class and in your reading. You will be in a better position to see how issues develop (the links, the contrasting elements or issues) and to identify the authorities in your discipline (who will be important to further reading). Periodic revision of the issues vital to your course will enable you to participate fully in the course and to be more effective in taking exams or completing assessment tasks. Spending half an hour each week rereading notes will save you hours of stress and study at the end of the semester.

NOTE-TAKING IN CLASS

Prepare for each class by skim reading the relevant reading material, taking note of key words and arguments. Some lecturers put up lecture notes on course websites for their students to refer to. These are sometimes brief but provide a valuable indication of the arguments that will be presented in class. Think about the issues presented and jot down any thoughts or questions in your notebook. Use your notes to guide your listening or questioning during classes.

Note-taking in class is different from taking notes from your reading material. In a class situation you need to use a number of skills intensively in a short period: listening, critical thinking, note-taking, writing and so on, as the lecturer passes from one point to another. Concentrate on the lecturer's argument and jot down the main points rather than attempting to write down every word. Intensive listening is an active process and the concentration level required can be difficult to maintain over an hour or more. Signalling phrases will normally provide a sense of the importance of the various parts of the material, allowing the audience to focus on what follows. Watch out for phrases such as these:

- 'Having gone through the background detail, it is important to note that . . .'
- 'There are three major issues I want to concentrate on . . .'
- 'I would like to draw your attention to . . .'
- 'You should consider the following arguments . . .'

Attempting to take down too much detail will distract you from the real purpose of listening and thinking in class. Class notes are more meaningful as a summary of the class than as a verbatim account. Also, beware of falling into the trap of copying down every overhead or slide. It is easy to be so busy copying them down that you do not concentrate on what the lecturer says, thus rendering your notes almost useless. Think about what is being said and take down the important points. If you feel that a slide would be important to your notes, ask the lecturer for a copy after class.

You will find as you progress in your studies that you develop abbreviations which help you jot down main issues quickly. Some common note-taking abbreviations are outlined in Appendix 4 to help you get started.

Figure 5.3 is an example of a page of lecture notes.

The presentation details, that is, the date, topic, lecturer's name and session number, are written at the top of the page. This information helps in keeping an organised record. The page is not crowded with lots of writing, allowing for the insertion of extra details later. Abbreviations are used when possible.

Figure 5.3 Example of class notes

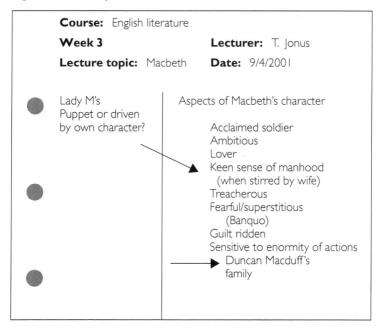

A good habit to develop, which will help you get the most out of your classes, is rereading your notes after each class. This facilitates memorisation of facts and guides your critical thinking. It also provides the ideal opportunity to check the sense of what you have written and add important details while they are still fresh in your mind. In doing this your notes become a valuable study tool, not just an exercise in note-taking.

Taking notes in a laboratory session or workshop

In practical classes, where you need to have a hands-on approach, you need to add watching and doing to the list of skills you employ. In these classes your note-taking will include a mixture of what your lecturer mentions and the interesting aspects or functions of the activities that you undertake. An organised, readily accessible notebook is important.

NOTE-TAKING AND THE WORD PROCESSOR

Some students elect to word process their notes, particularly for research projects. The word processor allows you to correct, make additions, rearrange, write comments in different colours, cut and paste and so on. However, a screen is not as easy to scan for information as a paper-based text. If you intend to rely on word-processed notes you need to be strict about organising files and disks. Ensure you always name a document with a meaningful title that reflects the content and the version you have written (first draft, second draft . . . final). Insert the name at the top of the document or in the footer so that the hard copy in your notebook gives the name of the computer file for easy reference later. If you are working on a project that has a number of sections it might help to assign a file to each chapter or section. *Always* back up your files on disk. Some students, particularly visual learners, find it helpful to use colour-coded disks, allotting a colour for each subject. Label each disk and file it immediately in a disk storage box so that it does not get lost amongst other items on your desk.

TAKING NOTES FROM TEXTS

Always consider the purpose of your reading before you start note-taking from a text. When reading in preparation for a written assignment keep the topic or questions clearly in mind to ensure you read appropriately and take relevant notes. Try not to be distracted by interesting but irrelevant information. Always record the original source of the information above your notes, fully and accurately. This will save time later and prevents accidental plagiarism (see p. 128).

Reading one section of a text at a time assists in the note-taking process. Concentrate on getting an overview, and on synthesising the main argument in your own words—don't allow yourself to be diverted by minor issues. Be active in your note-taking, having a pen and notebook ready whenever you read, whether you are on the bus or in the library. This way you can note down the main points easily, and any of your own thoughts as they come to mind. Use headings to organise and structure your notes to save yourself time and effort in accessing them later. Just thinking about the wording of headings can facilitate the process of synthesising main arguments.

PRESENTING YOUR NOTES

Well-organised and well-presented notes will give you an effective tool to assist in general course preparation, assignments and exams. Presentation techniques which facilitate note-taking effectiveness include: the linear method, mind-mapping and the margin-notes method.

Linear note-taking method

This method involves taking down information and organising it in a linear or systematic way. It lends itself well to recording facts as it relies heavily on headings and points arranged under each one. Figure 5.4 shows an example of this style.

Figure 5.4 Linear note-taking method

Study skills class: Note-taking

Lecturer: B. De Winton   15/5/2001

Good note-taking strategies:

1. Record complete source details at the top of the page
2. Leave adequate space to add points & ideas
3. Focus on the topic and record main points only
4. Write clearly

Reasons for note-taking:

1. Memory aid
2. Preparation for classes & exams
3. Practise in formulating ideas
4. Assists in making sense of ideas

Figure 5.5 Mind-mapping note-taking method

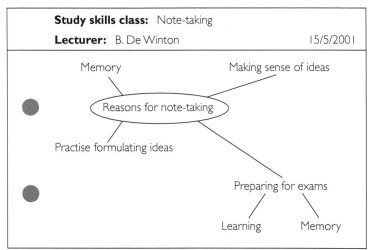

Mind-mapping method

Mind-mapping can be used to take notes from both reading and classes. This method is suited to concepts and the representation of ideas, and to the relationship between main ideas and supporting details. Figure 5.5 gives an example.

Margin-notes note-taking method

The margin-notes method involves ruling a generous margin on one side of the page where you can add your own notes, thoughts and questions alongside class or reading notes. Figure 5.6 gives an example. Margin notes are often combined with the linear method.

Figure 5.6 Margin-notes note-taking method

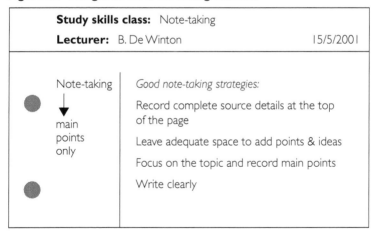

Synthesising the main arguments of your notes in a short summary is a good strategy which assists in recall of the main arguments and allows for easy referencing when the notes are called upon for assignment or exam preparation. Summarise your reading as you go along with a few lines in a special section at the beginning or end of your notebook. Summarising each paragraph (if the reading isn't too long) or section as you skim read will assist you in this process. Also summarise the main arguments presented in your classes, especially in lectures, that same evening or the morning after (while the ideas are still fresh). These summaries will provide an overview of the arguments which you will be able to turn to easily. Summaries can be highlighted with a coloured pen or framed in a box for easy identification.

RECORDING YOUR SOURCES

Taking clear, organised references as you study will make the whole process efficient and less frustrating. Having to track down the information later is a waste of time and might hold up the submission of an assignment. The appropriate method of recording sources will depend on how many sources you have. If there are only a few you can use a references record sheet or index cards. If you have many references because you are undertaking a large research project or a thesis, it might be worthwhile investigating the use of a computer program such as EndNote.

Figure 5.7 Example of an index card

Author name ———	De Fazio, Teresa **Date** 1999 **Call no.** 378.94DEF	
Title ———	*Studying in Australia: A Guide for International Students*	
Publisher details ———	Allen & Unwin, Sydney, NSW	
Description ———	Explores good study skills strategies for studying in Australia and understanding the Australian tertiary system. It covers:	
	culture shock	note-taking
	writing styles	reading
	exam preparation	tertiary system etc.

The references record sheet should have its own section in your notebook and will become your bibliography for an assignment. If you think you will use the same sources for a number of assignments, you might choose to organise a notebook just for the alphabetical collection of sources. Copy the blank references record sheet provided in Appendix 5 for your folder.

Index cards contain the same information as a record sheet but are set out differently. Your style may differ from the example given in Figure 5.7.

You will develop your skills as an active, critical reader as you take up opportunities throughout the course to question, and engage with, your reading material. Clear and relevant notes will become the working documents which you can call upon for the preparation of assignments, for exams or simply for memory prompts to prepare for a class.

✓ CHECKLIST: NOTE-TAKING

❑ Record appropriate, full details at the top of the page or in the margin for each reference item; include the date, source of information, page numbers, etc.

❑ Leave space so you can add your own points or ideas

❑ Focus on the topic and record only relevant, main points

❑ Think about how the ideas in your notes relate to information presented in the course

❑ Use abbreviations, but only those that you will remember

❑ Highlight key words and phrases

❑ Review your notes when you have finished to check whether anything has been omitted or is unclear

❑ Write up a brief summary of the notes

❑ Write clearly but do not fuss about being extra neat

❑ Never think that a writer has expressed things better than you can and end up copying down slabs of text; think about the central idea in the message and paraphrase it if need be (citing the source)

❑ Take care to use your own words, or carefully cite sources if you are quoting, so that you avoid the risk of plagiarism

❑ Keep all your notes in separate folders for each subject

❑ File notes as you go along

> **To write simply is as difficult as to be good.**
>
> Somerset Maugham

6

Developing your writing skills

Writing is but one aspect of entering into academic discourse. Through the development of a written argument you will be able to present what you know about an issue and your perspective on it. Written assignments demonstrate your ability to participate in a discipline's particular style of communicating; for instance, the humanities rely on essays whereas engineering relies heavily on reports, as do business and science (yet these disciplines each have their own style). There are a number of aspects to written communication, such as organising thoughts, understanding the writing conventions of your discipline, grammar, punctuation, vocabulary, dealing with jargon, using non-discriminatory language, finding your own style and academic tone. It is no wonder that we all find writing to be one of the most challenging aspects of the academic experience. This chapter takes you through various aspects and looks at how you can develop good writing skills.

REASONING AND WRITING

The first stage of your writing task involves reflection and reasoning. Your reasoning will make up your argument. Whether you are asked to write an essay, a research project or a short-answer question, the process is the same: carefully review the question and think about your response in terms of your critical thinking skills. Your strongest clues will come from **key phrases** or **key words** and **instruction words**, which will guide your reasoning process. Look at this example of an essay question:

<u>Why</u> should <u>school students</u> learn a <u>second language</u>?

 1500 words

The key words are underlined and the instruction word is circled. Appendix 6 explains a number of commonly used instruction words.

While you consider your main argument, think about your evidence—here your critical reading skills will be of value. In reviewing the question you need to think clearly about what is actually being asked, which means that you should consider the question from different perspectives. This will also lead you to decide on the style of writing that is required by the question— for instance, is it to be an argumentative, descriptive or analytical answer?

Our example poses a question which the essay writer is asked to *discuss*, thus the essay needs to focus on two elements:

• the rationale for second language learning; and
• the educational value of a second language for school learners.

The implicit message is that the writer needs to either support or reject the idea that second language learning is of value in the school curricula.

It is important to stay focused on the question and the different parts it may contain. It is sometimes easy to twist the argument around to what we think the question is asking, or what we feel comfortable answering. You need to be aware of this, as it might lead you to digress a little or even stray from the topic entirely. If you are unclear about the question (and sometimes, let's face it, lecturers do not always write the clearest questions) it is best to jot down some thoughts about what the question might be asking from you and make an appointment with your lecturer to ascertain whether you are on the right track.

CONSIDER YOUR ARGUMENT

The best place to start is with your own reactions. In this case the topic is asking you to discuss, that is, outline your stance, on the subject, whether you agree or not, or agree in part, and to provide relevant points as to the *reasoning* behind your stance. Remember the six inquiry questions we discussed in Chapter 2 (Who? Why? What? When? Where? How?), which will assist your reasoning or critical thinking. Reasoning may lie along the lines of exploring a number of details regarding the learning of second languages, giving some examples and drawing on other forms of evidence to support the notion or conclusion, for instance, that there *is* value in learning a second language. This essay does not have a large word limit, so it is much better to bring in a limited number of main points and discuss each one comprehensively than to touch on many points without dealing with any of them properly. Ensure that the points you choose to discuss are relevant to the topic and are not just of secondary interest.

CONSIDER YOUR AUDIENCE

It is important to consider who would be interested in reading your assignment. Your lecturer has given you a specific task so that you can demonstrate, firstly, your awareness of important issues on that topic, and secondly, that you can provide a purposeful, reasoned argument in a manner that is acceptable to a certain group of people (you might think of this as the practical training side of your course). For this example the interested people might be those involved in language education or in education in general. The audience might comprise of teachers, policy makers, parents and community representatives.

ORGANISING YOUR WRITING

Your writing will be structured according to the writing conventions of the document you are producing—for instance, a report has a different structure to an essay. Any document generally has three distinct main components in which the argument is explicated: the introduction, the body and the conclusion. We will deal with these three parts before turning to planning and writing up issues.

The introduction

The introduction, generally one paragraph, should tell the readers what to expect right from the beginning so that he or she will be able to make the connections necessary to follow the argument as it is evolved. The introduction's main purpose is to outline the direction of your writing (a direction which will depend on the instruction word) and will let the reader know whether, for instance, you will state your position or opinion on a particular argument (discuss), identify aspects of two particular issues (compare) or present the main ideas of a selected text (summarise). The introduction also serves to:

- provide any necessary background to the topic;
- point out the relevance of the argument to the discipline;
- explain why you selected a particular text or perspective;
- state your theoretical stance on a topic; and
- define key terms used in the written text.

In short, the introductory paragraph serves to capture the reader's attention by saying *what* will be talked about and *how* it will be talked about. You might summarise the main themes of the text and outline them in the order they are presented in the body of the assignment.

The body

The body of the assignment follows the introduction. Here your main ideas are presented clearly, with supporting arguments or evidence. You will be the best judge of how much evidence you need to include, though the assignment's word length will also guide you. Your reading and lecture notes will be of assistance here. Each idea should be dealt with in its own paragraph. A number of ideas in the one paragraph tends to confuse the reader. The next section describes the process of developing paragraphs based around a main idea and supporting details.

Paragraphing

When you are first developing your writing skills it is often helpful to start at the paragraph level before working up to the whole text. Paragraphs are units which discuss, explain, propose or contrast an idea, thus each paragraph should deal with only the one idea. There is no real word limit for a paragraph, so be wary of guides that prescribe a numerical approach. Paragraphs will vary in length according to the idea you are discussing, the detail in the supporting statements, your writing style and purpose. One- or two-sentence paragraphs should be used sparingly as such brevity generally does not allow for the *development* of an idea.

Each paragraph should include a sentence that outlines the main idea of that paragraph. This is called the *topic sentence*, and it can be placed at the beginning, middle or end of the paragraph depending on your writing style. The idea in the topic sentence is picked up and given more detail through supporting statements. These may include explanation, clarification, definition, example, drawing conclusions or showing cause and effect (of course, it is important to include all necessary citations here). If you are not certain where to place a topic sentence, put it at the beginning (most people do this anyway); here it not only guides the reader but also guides your writing.

A helpful exercise for formulating paragraphs is to read a newspaper article, or a chapter in a non-fiction textbook, one paragraph at a time. Summarise each paragraph in a few words in the margin. Done carefully, your summary should correspond to the topic sentence in that paragraph. (Be warned—not every paragraph has one; even published writers sometimes forget or confuse this all-important sentence.) Another common mistake is to have so many ideas lumped together that the topic sentence (or main idea) becomes confused.

By using the technique of linking paragraphs you will guide your reader from idea to idea, developing your argument as you work towards the conclusion. Linking paragraphs is done through the development of ideas so that one idea leads logically to another; this can be facilitated through the use of linking phrases or connectives to maintain reader focus. Firstly, linking two paragraphs can be done by pointing to the next idea at the end of a paragraph, or referring back to the previous idea at the beginning of the next paragraph. If the paragraphs are short, this linking technique may make your essay wordy and laborious to read. Secondly, connectives (or conjunctives) such as 'furthermore', 'in addition' and 'in contrast' can be used easily and efficiently to link paragraphs. (A list of connectives appears in Appendix 7.) Use these carefully; a common mistake is their overuse.

Figure 6.1 Using linking phrases

To signal the start of an idea	• Use topic sentences • The main argument involves ... • The issue centres around ... • The arguments are based on ...
To signal a move to the next idea	• So far the arguments raised have been centred around ... so we can now turn our attention to ... • I have discussed the issues regarding ... so will now turn to ... • We've seen how ... and will now investigate ... • Having a familiarity with the issues just outlined will facilitate our understanding of ... • On the other hand, ...
To signal the conclusion of one idea	• In short, I have demonstrated ... • In brief, the issues demonstrate that ... • All of this points to ... • So, we can see that ... • Thus, it is clear that ... • Having understood that ..., it is reasonable to assume that ...
Sequencing	• Firstly, ... secondly, ... thirdly, ...
The use of connectives	See Appendix 6

The conclusion

The conclusion is an important paragraph that is too often over-looked in the relief of finding that the bulk of the assignment has been organised. It is just as important to have a strong ending to the argument as it is to have a strong beginning. The conclusion should review the points mentioned in the body by bringing them to a logical conclusion and linking the whole argument with the title, thus bringing it full circle. The conclusion is meant to leave the reader with something to think about without intro-ducing any new ideas. It should strengthen your argument simply and, in a sense, be your last word.

PLANNING WRITTEN ASSIGNMENTS

It is vital that you devise a writing plan for each assignment. The plan is a valuable tool that will assist you to maintain your focus on the topic and organise your thoughts in a logical structure. Some students write up detailed plans, which they find makes the writing process quicker; for others the drafting of the written assignment attracts the most time. The strategy you choose will depend on both your writing style and the demands of the assignment. Any plan will probably change as your thoughts and your writing up evolve. Do not feel that a plan is a sacred document that must not be tampered with—rather, it is a document to guide and facilitate the directions of your thoughts and the writing-up process overall. Jotting down approximate word lengths for each paragraph may be helpful. As you will generally be expected to demonstrate familiar-ity with the main arguments presented by the authorities on your topic, your class and reading notes will be of value. Figure 6.2 outlines a sample essay plan.

The checklist for drafting and editing provided at the end of the chapter will assist you with your written assignments. Good planning will also help you avoid pitfalls of writing, such as:

Figure 6.2 Sample essay plan

Question (including word length)

Position/stance or argument (word length . . .):

Main idea 1 (word length . . .):

Supporting arguments (including notes to references you have found of interest):
1.
2.
3.

Main idea 2 (word length . . .):

Supporting arguments (including notes to references you have found of interest)
1.
2.
3.

Main idea 3 (word length . . .):

Supporting arguments (including notes to references you have found of interest):
1.
2.
3.

Concluding remarks (word length . . .):

- digressing from the main idea;
- trying to say too much;
- repeating the same idea;
- structuring the assignment in an illogical or confusing order;
- padding out an argument;

- omitting important points; and
- failing to cite all your sources.

When you are thinking about what to write, remember to keep focused on the six inquiry questions. For instance, *who* said *what* and *why*? *How* do you come to a certain conclusion? *Where* is the evidence and in *what* context is it relevant? *Why* do you think so? *When* or in *what* circumstances is something relevant?

GETTING STARTED

Writing anxiety is common and most people will face it at some time. Feeling stressed about writing is hardly surprising when you are not used to writing for academic purposes; you may feel you are faced with an utterly daunting task. Even professional writers sometimes find that ideas dry up for a while (the famous 'writer's block'), but then another idea will come along and get them going again. Your task is to *start* writing; once you start, your thoughts will lead to other thoughts and the writing process will develop. Stop reordering your desk, stop reading on the topic, stop sharpening your pencils—just start writing. It sounds too simple, but it does work.

There are a number of strategies you can try to get yourself started. Begin with the section or the idea which you feel most confident about, and just write, putting down words, phrases, terms, half sentences, even confused sentences, in whatever order they come to mind. Spending time on planning also helps in overcoming writer's block. Jot down ideas as they come—and believe me, they will come. Don't worry about topic sentences or supporting statements at this stage; don't concern yourself with spelling or grammar either; at this point, they may only add to your anxiety. Many people find the word processor is a helpful writing tool because it is interactive: the blinking cursor, the ease of cutting and pasting, can prove motivating.

Concentrate on getting the thoughts out of your head and onto paper or screen. Slowly the ideas will begin to flow, and so will your writing. You may end up discarding quite a bit at the end of a session, but you will also have some good material. Do as much as you can in one session, leave off for a couple of days, then return to it. You might find that some helpful ideas have come into your head as you have gone about your other activities, which will make the writing process easier when you sit back at your desk.

If you still find that you are getting nowhere, that things seem too difficult, then it is time to seek assistance, either from a learning support person or your lecturer. Sometimes just discussing the problem can be extremely helpful.

DRAFTING AND EDITING

Drafting is an important and necessary step in the writing-up stage. Some of the world's most famous novelists work on many different drafts. Even with a detailed writing plan chances are you will need at least two so allow time in your schedule. The number of drafts you end up with will depend on the way you have tackled the task, your writing style, and how long it takes to get your thoughts down on paper in a way that is coherent, logical and pertinent. Once you have a draft, leave it for a few days while you attend to other study tasks. The lapse of time often gives you the 'distance' you need to get a fresh perspective on what you have written. In the end this makes the writing process easier and more effective as, in a sense, you need to critically analyse your own writing.

When you go back to the draft, check to see that you have supported your claims, that each idea has been explained clearly and that you have made the necessary connections between ideas. Consider whether you need to do more research, or to resequence your ideas to develop a more logical argument. A quick, efficient way of checking on the logical sequencing and development of ideas is to summarise each paragraph in a few lines in the margin. This summary should match the idea reflected by the topic sentence. Thus, this strategy will highlight whether your topic sentence is clear and whether each paragraph concentrates on one idea. If more than one idea is included you may have to split the paragraph and do some rewriting. It is difficult sometimes to cut out something that you have anguished over for hours, but be prepared to do so.

Leave the revised draft for a few more days, and repeat the process. The checklist on aspects of drafting at the end of the chapter is there to help you.

Editing is a different process to drafting, though some confuse the two. Editing involves checking for more superficial elements. You should check spelling, grammar, punctuation, that all sources have been cited, and aspects of presentation (are heading sizes appropriate? Does the table of contents contain all the headings in the text?). Presentation is important. Don't allow all that hard work getting the content right go to waste because your presentation is shoddy. Follow the editing checklist at the end of this chapter before submitting your work.

CITING SOURCES

Drawing on sources is integral to the way in which academic argument evolves, which is why it needs to be done carefully. The particular referencing style you need to use will be dictated by your lecturer, and all you need to do is follow the convention in a formulaic manner (see Chapter 9). The ways in which citations are integrated into your argument, however, are the same for any convention or text type.

You need to think carefully about how possible citations from your sources will work within the context of your writing. Quotations should support your ideas, so choose them carefully, considering their value to the argument you are presenting. They can be included:

- as the reason you followed a particular line of investigation or argument;
- as strong evidence for your viewpoint (even if in opposition);
- to indicate what else is happening or has been found in the field of study (quoting statistics, for instance); or
- to set the scene or background for your argument.

Your writing should not be full of citations with only a sprinkling of your own words; it should be the other way around. To give weight to your argument, draw on authorities in the area rather than citing just anyone who has had something to say on the topic. Be certain that you understand what you are citing, and that the context in which the author was writing actually works to build your argument rather than confuse it, or worse, work against it. If you come across a quote which seems to encapsulate an idea well and which will add emphasis to your main argument, you might choose to use a direct quote, either wholly or in part.

Use inverted commas ('. . .') to set off the quotation, which should follow the exact wording, spelling and punctuation of the original text; for example:

> Elbow (1981, pp.16–17) discusses the concept of freewriting as producing 'syntactic coherence and verbal energy' which motivates and directs the process itself.

Quotes of three lines or more should be separated from your writing by a line space, above and below, indented and single spaced; there is no need to add inverted commas when quotes are set out this way. The example below shows how this is done; it also shows how you use three dots with a space either side to represent words omitted from the original.

> Writing can be viewed as a complicated process, as suggested by Elbow (1981, p.7):
>
> > Writing calls on two skills that are so different that they usually conflict with each other: creating and criticizing. In other words, writing calls on the ability to create words and ideas out of yourself, but it also calls on the ability to criticize them in order to decide which ones to use ... these opposite mental processes can go on at the same time.

Sometimes an original quote needs to be modified to fit into the text you are writing, particularly in terms of grammar or for clarification. Whenever you modify text your modifications should be included in square brackets; for example:

> Elbow (1981, p.37) claims that when one has '*lots* of time for revising [one] tend[s] to finish with something longer than ... expected'.

You may choose to paraphrase a quotation, particularly if the quotation is long and wordy. Such indirect quotations appear in the text you are writing and have the advantage of not breaking up the flow of the writing. Rephrasing an idea might be set out like this:

> Elbow (1981, p.7) refers to the process of writing as one where the writer needs to come up with words while making judgements on the validity of these words.

When referring to a general idea rather than a particular one, you can cite the work without inserting a particular page number; for example:

> Elbow (1981) outlines the freewriting process as one that may assist in unblocking the blocked writer.

Figure 6.3 presents some examples of phrases useful for introducing indirect quotations.

All the works cited in your paper should appear as full citations in either the references list or the bibliography, following the conventions of the required referencing system, as demonstrated in Chapter 9.

Figure 6.3 Useful phrases for introducing indirect quotations

Luca points out ...	Devid suggests ...
Isabella claims ...	Totto demonstrates ...
Gianni observes ...	Lina refers to ...
According to Giulia, ...	Nguyen recommends that ...
Doris reports that ...	Poppi outlines ...
Finian defines ... as ...	Gemi proposes that ...
Research by Tessa indicates that ...	Sohimi notes ...
Boceli argues ...	Wingen writes ...
In a study by the Bureau of ... it is suggested that ...	

ACADEMIC TONE

Some students complain that they cannot express themselves in the intellectual manner they perceive is required by academic writing. Academic writing in general is more formal in style than speech. These days, luckily, the emphasis is not on sounding so intellectual that no one understands what you are saying, but on expressing your ideas in a clear, logical and coherent manner. It is more important to be comfortable with your own spoken or written language and to concentrate on the message than to use fancy or pretentious phrases. Where jargon was once commonly used, it is now seen as being an impediment to understanding. You will be required to know, and use accurately, discipline-specific language but not in a way that makes you sound pedantic. Jargon and fancy phrases used for their own sake are not going to get you those extra marks: content and clear expression will. However, stay clear of colloquialisms or slang; if they are required, set them off with italics or enclose them in quotation marks. Write words out in full rather than using abbreviations.

USING NON-DISCRIMINATORY LANGUAGE

As part of the growing awareness of equity issues it is generally accepted that non-discriminatory language should be used in spoken and written communication. Any words or phrasing suggesting bias, stereotyping or prejudice should be avoided, particularly in issues concerning race, gender, religious background or profession. Figure 6.4 gives an example of a phrase using discriminatory language and demonstrates how it can be rewritten to avoid the use of such language.

Figure 6.4 Treating gender bias

Gender-biased statement:
A doctor's role is a complex one. He needs to be a medical expert, a psychologist, a counsellor, a social worker . . .

Gender-free statements:
1. *A doctor's role is a complex one in that it entails being a medical expert, a psychologist, a counsellor, a social worker . . .*
2. *A doctor's role is a complex one. She/He needs to be a medical expert, a psychologist, a counsellor, a social worker . . .*
3. *Doctors have a complex role. They need to be medical experts, psychologists, counsellors, social workers . . .*

The three gender-free statements demonstrate the use of, firstly, the continuation of the passive sense of the phrase (neither gender is alluded to), secondly, the specific detailing of both genders (she/he) and thirdly, the use of the plural.

GETTING ASSISTANCE WITH YOUR WRITING

Keep in mind that you can always see someone regarding your writing. Your lecturer may be willing to go through writing plans or drafts to check that you are on the right track, or that you have structured your text according to the correct discipline conventions. You might need advice from a study skills adviser on such matters as style, getting started, structure and expression. Some students have the impression that only students with English problems, or the not so capable, see study skills advisers. Wrong! Even lecturers get advice from study skills advisers.

GETTING FEEDBACK

Most lecturers (not all, unfortunately) will provide helpful feedback on your finished assignments. You should take note of any comments as they will help you with your next task, much more, in fact, than the end score. Such comments will provide information on lecturer expectations on the way you structure your argument, use evidence, develop your arguments, present your tasks or express your ideas. Comments are meant to be constructive rather than personal or critical, so concentrate positively on the issues identified by the lecturer. The checklists appearing throughout this book reflect lecturer expectations on most aspects of written work. Keep in mind, however, that some lecturers emphasise certain aspects over others. If you do not receive detailed feedback on your assessment tasks, it is important to ask for it. This will not be seen as impertinent, if done politely; rather, it will demonstrate your keenness to do well. While some lecturers tend to give up on detailed feedback because too many students show interest only in the end mark, they are usually quite keen to provide a motivated student with constructive and detailed feedback.

Developing your writing skills is an ever-evolving, ever-challenging process. It takes a lot of reflection, questioning and planning before even getting to the practical act of putting words down on paper. Viewing the writing process as a series of steps will assist you in approaching your writing tasks methodically. This does not mean that your writing will end up being rigid and boring. It should, however, help you to develop a clear understanding of the writing task before you.

✓ CHECKLIST: DRAFTING AND EDITING

Drafting

❑ Have you answered the question?

❑ Does the introduction indicate what the main argument of the document will be?

❑ Has the text answered the question?

❑ Have all the necessary main points been included?

❑ Are the supporting arguments clear?

❑ Do the main ideas stand out?

❑ Are the ideas clear for the reader? If not, what

Editing

❑ Are there any spelling errors?

❑ Is the grammar accurate?

❑ Is the punctuation used accurately?

❑ Have all the appendices been included?

❑ Are the margins the appropriate size?

❑ Is the assignment double spaced if required?

❑ Have you used words of whose meaning you are not certain? (If so, check and substitute if necessary.)

changes should be made (for instance, add examples or diagrams or rewrite the section)?

❑ Does each paragraph contain one clear and recognisable idea rather than several? If not, the ideas may need to be dealt with in separate paragraphs.

❑ Does the argument flow from one paragraph to another?

❑ Is there any needless digression to delete?

❑ Is the word count allocated appropriately?

❑ Are the headings representative of the idea in the paragraph(s) that follow?

❑ Are the paragraphs in a logical sequence?

❑ Is there repetition? If so, which part should be deleted?

❑ Have you defined any special terms used?

❑ Are colloquialisms or slang included? (These may need to be re-phrased.)

❑ Is any discriminatory language included? (The wording may need to be reviewed.)

❑ Is the bibliography or references list set out according to the referencing system adopted?

❑ Have all the sources been cited appropriately?

❑ Have all the references cited in the text been included in the references list or bibliography?

❑ Are the headings clear, not too wordy?

❑ Is the cover page presentable?

❑ Are page numbers included?

❑ Is a list of tables/figures included?

❏ Are the sources integrated into the main argument of the text?

❏ Are they relevant to the argument?

❏ Have you avoided discriminatory language?

❏ Is there a sense of audience awareness?

❏ Does the conclusion bring together the main ideas of the argument?

❏ Does it leave the reader with something to think about?

❏ Are tables/figures numbered appropriately?

❏ Is a brief description of each table/figure included?

❏ Do you have hard copy and disk copy prepared and stored away safely in case the lecturer's dog eats your assignment?

> True ease in writing
> comes from art, not
> chance,
> As those move easiest
> who have learn'd to
> dance.
>
> Alexander Pope, *Essay on Criticism*

7

Essay writing

Sitting down to write an essay can often be a daunting task. You may not have written one for years, or ever. You may never have written an academic one. The conventions and expectations of structure and argument may be unfamiliar. As there are a number of steps in the process of academic essay writing, as always, organisation is a major factor. Efficient organisation will help you avoid the common traps of essay writing: irrelevant points, illogical sequencing, digression, repetition, not attending to the word limit, poor referencing. This chapter outlines the steps involved in essay planning and writing and explores different essay types, paragraphing and the drafting process. There is a worked example as an illustration of the process.

ESSAY TYPES

The previous chapter mentioned the tendency for each discipline to rely on its own style of written text. Essays also differ in perspective depending on the purpose of the argument. The three main essay types you should know about are the argumentative, the descriptive and the analytical.

The argumentative essay

This essay style concentrates on presenting an analysis of an argument. Using this style you would present a reasoned, clear discussion on a topic that outlines a main argument and supporting evidence in order to persuade the reader to see your argument as a reasonable one. Your lecturer would look for evidence that you are able to state a clear point of view and can present a reasoned discussion that draws on supporting evidence and examples. Your material needs to be authoritative and reliable if it is to be effective in persuading the reader. It must be reasoned in terms of considering any opposing arguments and demonstrating why they are not as reliable or logical as those you are presenting.

The descriptive essay

This type of essay is centred around describing an event, a situation, a method or a hypothesis. Generally your lecturer would look for evidence that you can identify the most relevant issues pertaining to the topic and that you can present them in a clear and accurate manner. An important part of this descriptive process is indicating the significance of these main issues, the reasons they are so important.

The analytical essay

The purpose of the analytical essay is to compare and/or evaluate theories, arguments, models, methodologies, a writer's style or some other aspect indicated by the essay question. Your ability to see points of similarity and contrast and to evaluate their significance is an important feature of this essay type. Your lecturer would look for evidence that you are able to identify relevant issues or relationships between the aspects you focus on in your essay. You may also be required to present your own opinion of the value of the aspects evaluated once you have presented your analysis and outline your reasons for holding that opinion.

WRITING UP AN ESSAY PLAN

Viewing the different steps in writing up an essay as a process will help you develop both your planning and your writing skills. The steps are outlined with a worked example as illustration.

Analysing the topic

The first step in any assignment is to analyse the topic carefully by identifying the **key words** and the **instruction word**. You must have a clear picture of what you are required to do, otherwise you risk answering what you *think* is the question rather than the question itself.

<u>Why</u> should <u>school students</u> learn a <u>second language</u>?

 Discuss.   <u>1500</u> words

The key words and the instruction word have been highlighted. The question requires an argumentative essay which should persuade or dissuade the reader regarding the value of second language learning, thus a position or opinion is demanded.

Clarifying your argument

Once you have a clear idea of what the question is asking of you, think about your immediate response in terms of your stance, opinion or argument and write this down in two or three lines underneath the question. You might find it beneficial to revise this response after the next step, but it will serve to frame the initial direction of your essay planning and research.

One possible response might be:

It is important to include learning a second language in the school curriculum for a number of reasons: cognitive development, the promotion of cultural awareness and the increased vocational opportunities which have a beneficial flow on-effect on this country's role in the global context.

Brainstorming

The next step is getting points down on paper. An initial brainstorming session is often very useful. It can save you from wasting time reading irrelevant material as it will help you focus your opinions and direct your reading. Admittedly, the brainstorming process is easier with some essay topics than with others. Sometimes it will seem that you are overflowing with ideas, at other times it can be difficult to get even one word down. Sometimes talking with classmates, workmates, friends or family can make it easier to formulate and articulate your ideas.

If you feel blocked, try getting ideas down on paper as they come to mind; don't be concerned about sequencing at this stage. Try dissecting the question and just start writing, even if it means you end up listing a number of related questions which you will need to investigate through further reflection and reading. These points or questions will help you with the next step. The mindmap in Figure 7.1 illustrates the process of brainstorming.

If you are really stuck for ideas do the reading first, then the brainstorming.

Figure 7.1 Brainstorming mindmap

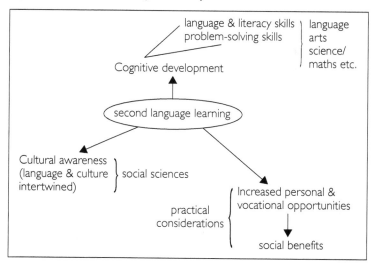

Taking notes

The next step is to read on the topic and take notes. Your notes will often mirror what you have already thought, providing useful evidence in support of your position. While you are reading you will add, delete or rearrange your notes as ideas spring to mind. You do not need to put these points in any order at this stage—concentrate on the topic, thinking and reading critically. The quality of your notes will dictate the efficiency and organisation of the whole writing process. It is important to jot down relevant notes, rather than allowing yourself to be side-tracked by interesting but irrelevant points.

As you take notes, remember to make careful note of the source; jot down referencing details in your notes and include full citation details in your recording system, to save time when you come to working on the bibliography later. Points for the example essay question might appear as in Figure 7.2

Figure 7.2 Example of essay notes

- language ability increases cognitive ability and problem solving skills in particular (Ben Zeev, 1977)
- Gardner's (1993) language skills not just related to linguistic intelligence but also logico-mathematical intelligence. Imp. to all areas of the school curriculum (e.g. maths, sciences)
- learning a second language makes it easier to learn others due to cognitive flexibility and awareness of how language works. Cook (1991, p.135)—'children who know a second language are better at separating semantic from phonetic aspects of words, at tasks involving classification, at tests of creativity; they have sharper awareness of language,' → first language literacy

Planning your essay: the body

Drawing up a plan or outline for your essay may take a couple of drafts, but once you get this part right you will be well on the way to writing up a good essay. Having a plan means that you are less likely to digress or to succumb to a mental block. It also means that any further reading and, certainly, your writing will be argued in a logical sequence. Review your points and you should see several patterns of thought emerging, that is, certain main ideas will stand out from supporting evidence. Underline these main ideas as headings, then group relevant supporting evidence underneath. You will then have various chunks of an essay. Headings are not normally used in essays, unlike reports, but they are very useful in essay planning. You will find that some of the headings serve as prompts for topic sentences. The main ideas should be identified clearly as points. As you go through the process of organising the body of the essay, discard any irrelevant or repetitive points.

Once you have grouped your ideas, it is time to put them in order. You might even cut up each set of ideas and arrange the bits of paper on your desk, putting them in a different order until you come up with the best logical sequence. The ideas should be sequenced to provide an appropriate emphasis on each main point, and so that each idea builds up to producing the whole picture (argument) for the reader. You will be able to develop each of these ideas into paragraphs when you write out the essay. Remember: one paragraph, one idea. At this stage, too, you may wish to allot a certain number of words to each section as a rough guide. This will help you think about emphasising important points without going over the limit.

Your plan might now look like the plan in Figure 7.3.

Figure 7.3 Example of an essay plan

Essay question:
Why should school students learn a second language?
Discuss.   1500 words

Main argument:
Learning a second language facilitates general cognitive development:
→ processing skills important for all problem-solving situations.
→ understanding of how language works, patterns, structures, rules, forms, exceptions etc. thus, 2nd language learning also relevant to whole of language arts area.

Supporting arguments:
Processing skills
• Research indicates that processing skills in terms of logic and reasoning are enhanced through second language learning which in turn facilitates general problem solving (Ben Zeev, 1977).

- Gardner (1993) suggests that language skills not just related to linguistic intelligence but also logico-mathematical intelligence
  → imp. to all areas of the school curriculum (maths, sciences).

Language skill enhancement
- Knowing a second language brings understanding of first language functions → recognised by many researchers and commentators including Cook (1991, p.135) who, summarising research into the area, declares that 'children who know a second language are better at separating semantic from phonetic aspects of words, at tasks involving classification, at tests of creativity; they have sharper awareness of language'.
- the implications of this are: better standard of 1st language literacy.
- generally recognised that knowing two languages, having brought about an understanding of how language works, facilitates the acquisition of more languages.

Main argument:
Value of second language learning related to building socio-cultural awareness. Relevant to social sciences and of broad educational value.

Supporting arguments:
- Language and culture inextricably intertwined, e.g. word for snow, concept of siesta, sayings (traditions, values, history).
- Knowledge of a different culture facilitates the ability to interpret aspects of society & culture from different perspectives, e.g. Japanese regard for 'keeping face'—language as a 'social activity' (Edwards 1995).
- It allows the enjoyment of living in or visiting another country.
- Understanding facilitates integration into a foreign culture whether for short or long stay, comfort levels increased due to not feeling so isolated, foreign.
- (Cook 1991, p.146) 'Regardless of the actual language that is being learnt, it is often held to be beneficial for the students to understand

a foreign culture for its own sake.' ➡ broad educational value.

➡ International relations and student exchange programs make up a considerable proportion of study activities, gives the educational experience relevance and context (DEET, 2000)

Main argument:

Practical side of education to lead to vocational opportunities, preparation for future choices. Knowing a second language may lead to increased vocational opportunities and economic development particularly in an era of globalisation.

If we view schools as important to our country's general social and economic initiatives then languages have an important role in training students for communication and intercultural proficiency.

Supporting arguments:

- Globalisation means that countries are becoming more dependent on each other, that work opportunities are not limited by place, rather by skills, so having some fluency in a second language increases opportunities to work in a chosen field in different countries.
- In order to build economic bridges it is important to communicate, learning a second language provides direct and personal links when building such bridges.
- Tasm. Education Dept. (2000, p.1) 'Why learn languages other than English'—points out that a second language provides more vocational options which has a flow-on effect in terms of social benefits, leading to this country's integration 'as a powerful and dynamic member of the world community'.

The introduction and conclusion

At this stage the introduction and conclusion have not been outlined. While some students find it easier to attend to these sections in their logical order, I find that many others benefit from throwing themselves into the crux of the argument and getting this organised before writing up the introduction and conclusion. In fact, once the body is planned out well, these two sections almost 'write themselves'.

The introduction should capture the attention of the reader, stating your argument clearly and how you will develop it. The conclusion, on the other hand, should leave the reader with something to think about without bringing in any new details, instead bringing together the aspects of the argument you have presented without providing a summary.

In our essay example the introduction and conclusion might include the points shown in Figure 7.4.

Figure 7.4 Example of introduction and conclusion

Introduction:
Proposition: There is value in including second language learning in primary and secondary school studies.
This essay will concentrate on three main arguments:
- intellectual and linguistic enrichment
- development of cultural awareness
- enhancement of personal vocational opportunities & leading to benefit to the country

Conclusion:
Learning a second language is an asset personally and socio-economically.
➔ Promotes brain power, cultural enlightenment & understanding, vocational mobility which in turn leads to promoting this country's role in global community.
2nd lang. learning supports & extends skills and process of broad curriculum.
Language is a social activity and language learning a social concern, reflected in the school curriculum.

DRAFTING THE ESSAY

The next stage is to draft the essay, drawing on the plan you have devised. The final stage involves editing it. In writing up the first draft use topic sentences that relay the main idea of each paragraph, making sure they stand out from the supporting details or evidence. Express your ideas, avoiding complicated phrases as much as possible; concentrate on clarity of meaning. (You can work on grammar and expression in the next draft.) At the end of each paragraph lead on to the idea represented in the following paragraph to create a linear and logical structure.

Once you have completed the first draft leave it for a day or two if time permits. The perspective of distance will help you to evaluate it critically. Reread the draft a paragraph at a time, summarising the main ideas in the margin. This helps to ensure that there is an identifiable topic sentence in each paragraph, and one main idea instead of many. Ensure that each supporting detail relates to the main idea and is argued in a relevant, clear and logical manner. Check for omissions, digressions or repetitions and for a sense of connection between the paragraphs as the argument is built up.

The number of drafts you write will depend on your judgement; there is no magical figure but you will need at least two. Once the drafting process is completed you should proof or edit your work, reviewing it against the detailed checklist in the previous chapter. Figure 7.5 summarises the essay writing process.

It is important not to rush the essay-writing process. Instead, take time to do some critical thinking about the topic and how you will tackle the task; it is also valuable to approach your task with an attitude of distance, so that you can maintain a level of critical analysis that will facilitate your drafting and editing process.

Figure 7.5 Steps in essay writing

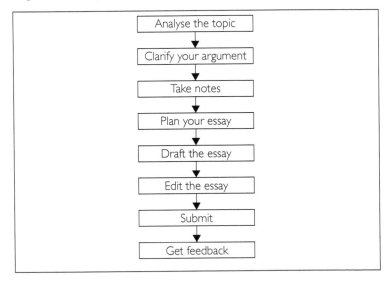

> **An intellectual is someone whose mind watches itself.**
>
> Albert Camus

8

Report writing

As part of your studies you may be required to write reports. While you may be used to writing or reading reports as part of your employment duties, workplace reports may differ considerably from those written for academic purposes. Reports also differ in style, format and content depending on the discipline, so it pays to check lecturer expectations. This chapter outlines some fundamental aspects of report writing and takes you through general differences in format, describing the general features of report writing and detailing the differences between business and scientific reports. Research reports are different again; they are totally academic in nature and normally undertaken at postgraduate level. They are dealt with separately in Chapter 11.

THE ROLE OF A REPORT

Reports are different to essays in terms of their objective and basically inform through the presentation of facts. In this sense the academic report is the same as a workplace report in that it generally presents facts to a reader who may not be aware of them but needs the information to make a decision or carry out a task. Essays demonstrate knowledge by presenting or juxtaposing arguments. A report can:

- describe a situation or problem;
- identify a problem;
- explain activities or a chosen course of action;
- record activities;
- analyse a process or product; or
- investigate a situation, idea or course of action.

Both essays and reports are written with a particular audience in mind (see Chapter 6). The brief for an essay is wider in scope than for a report, whose intent is narrower and certainly more functional. This is why an important component of the report is the recommendations section. This chapter provides an explanation of the main components of reports for scientific and business subjects, where they are most commonly used; the components of a general report are also explained, providing a useful guide for report-writing in any discipline, along with a checklist to guide your report preparation.

THE FORMAT OF A REPORT

Title page

This is the first page of your report and needs to include your name, the title, the date submitted, who the report is submitted to and the subject or course name. As with any document produced for submission, it pays to take a little extra care and make a good first impression by producing a professional, but not elaborate, title page.

Table of contents

A report that contains a number of sections should include a table of contents that lists the headings of each section and subsection with their corresponding page numbers. This permits the reader to gain a good overview of the report's components and how it is structured overall. Appendices should also appear in this list, with their titles. The appendices are not numbered by page. Standard page numbers (1, 2, 3 . . .) are used in the body of the report, roman numerals (i, ii, iii . . .) for such pages as the title page, table of contents, list of figures and tables and the executive summary.

List of tables or figures

Under the headings *List of tables* and *List of figures*, list tables and figures by number, with the table heading or figure caption and the pages on which they appear. This allows the reader to refer quickly to a particular item. Figure 8.1 gives an example of this page.

Figure 8.1 List of figures

List of figures	
1.1 Birth rates in 1998	p. 4
1.2 Birth rates, females, in 1998	p. 5
1.3 Birth rates, males, in 1998	p. 6
2.1 Comparison of female and male birth rates in 1998	p. 10
3.1 Expected birth rates in 2005	p. 15
3.2 Expected birth rates, females, in 2005	p. 16
3.3 Expected birth rates, males, in 2005	p. 16

Synopsis/Executive summary/Abstract

These three names all refer to the same thing, a section which provides an overall picture of the report. It includes a summary of the report's objectives, main points, conclusions and recommendations. This is done to give the reader a clear idea of what the report discusses, and particularly its highlights, before it is even read. This section is usually no longer than a page and can be written last to reflect the substance of the report exactly.

Introduction

At first glance, the introduction might seem to replicate the section just discussed, but it normally covers the four aspects of *why, who, how* and *what*. Firstly, it should include a statement of the objective(s) of the report—*why* it has been written. Here you should explain the relevance or importance of the topic and what you are attempting to demonstrate. Secondly, there should be a statement clarifying its authorisation, that is, *who* the report is being written for. Thirdly, a brief statement on *how* the data or information was gathered (the methodology), whether through interviews, surveys, literature or some other method. Finally, the introduction should indicate *what* the limitations of the report are, providing the reader with an outline of what has or has not been covered. Thus, the introduction should give the reader a clear idea of what is contained in the whole document.

Body of the report

This is the section where you include all the necessary information, any important background information, and any findings, consequences and/or events that have a bearing on the objective of the report. For instance, if the objective is to propose a particular course of action, methodology or perspective, you need to present arguments in this section that fulfil this objective.

This part of the document contains sections and subsections, each with numbered headings. Take a little time in considering the headings you will use: do they reflect the content of that section, are they 'catchy', are they succinct? Good planning is just as important in writing reports as for any other document. Planning and drafting, dealt with in Chapter 6, are important aspects of report writing. The language used in reports is commonly very straightforward. Tables, figures, graphs, charts and lists of points are good ways of presenting and illustrating facts. Remember to refer to figures and tables in the body of the text, as explained in the section below.

Setting out figures and tables

All immediately relevant diagrams, figures, graphs and tables should be included in the body of the report; those that are of supplementary value can be included in the appendices (each on a separate page) and referred to in the text. When you refer to a figure or table it is important that you explain clearly what it demonstrates. You must cite the original text if you obtained it from sources other than your own data collection. For ease of identification, as part of its heading each figure or table should be numbered according to the section in which it is included. Below it there should be a single-sentence, clear, brief explanation of what the table or figure demonstrates, which again includes its number (tables and figures should be numbered consecutively in separate sequences). The explanation is usually written in a slightly smaller font. Figure 8.2 gives an example of a graph which is the first to appear in the fourth section of a report.

Methodology

A vital part of the report is an explanation of how you carried out the investigation, a description of any equipment used, and your rationale for using a particular method of investigation. This is the methodology section, which needs to be clear and detailed to the point where another person can easily follow the instructions

Figure 8.2 Setting out of a graph

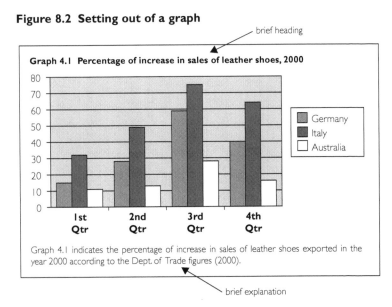

brief heading

Graph 4.1 Percentage of increase in sales of leather shoes, 2000

Germany
Italy
Australia

Graph 4.1 indicates the percentage of increase in sales of leather shoes exported in the year 2000 according to the Dept. of Trade figures (2000).

brief explanation

to replicate your approach (particularly in a scientific report). It is helpful to read other reports in your discipline to get an idea of the accepted style and approach.

Results

This section should outline the results of your research. Clearly explain what you have found and in what way your findings are significant or not. Again, tables and figures can be useful for demonstration purposes, particularly if they are statistically based. In the next section you will discuss the implications of these findings.

Discussion

Here you are expected to link the aims of the research and your findings, and the ways in which your findings are of interest. This means you need to analyse your findings in terms of the information presented in the body of the report, without bringing in any new information. Discuss why you believe you obtained these results, and any interesting points that have come out of your research—that is, discuss the significance of each of your findings. This demonstrates both that you are thinking objectively as a researcher and that you are able to view your work in terms of possible limitations or errors, which are outlined in the next section.

Recommendations and limitations

On the basis of the research undertaken, the researcher is often in a good position to make recommendations on future directions or actions, which should be outlined clearly in this section of the report. Any limitations of the study can be identified here as well, enabling other researchers to take them into account when carrying out further research into the area. For instance, a report on computerised educational systems might make recommendations as to which system, or combination of systems, is appropriate in a given educational setting. It may also include a statement regarding the small scale of the research and noting the need to carry out the same research on a larger scale to gain a more realistic picture. Recommendations need to be realistic, feasible and action-oriented, and are most usefully presented in order of importance.

Conclusions

This short section draws together the main points of each section of the report. It should not be just a summary but pull together all the threads of the report, particularly the key findings. It can include a number of listed points, with main conclusions appearing first. The conclusions need to be contextualised in terms of the report's objectives, as set out in the introduction.

Reference list/Endnotes

Here you should list all the sources used in preparing the report, using the reference system required by your lecturer. Chapter 9 outlines the various systems for citing both paper-based and online resources.

Appendices

This section includes supplementary information that is useful to the study but which is not appropriately placed in the body because it would interrupt the reader's attention. Here you might include extra tables, newspaper articles, copies of questionnaires used, letters, brochures and so on, each set out clearly with a title and arranged in the order they are referred to in the text. Information presented in the appendices should be relevant, not just added superfluously.

Figure 8.3 Sections of scientific and business reports

Scientific report:	Business report:
Title page	Title page
Table of Contents	Table of Contents
List of Figures (if relevant)	List of Figures (if relevant)
List of Tables or Illustrations (if relevant)	List of Tables or Illustrations (if relevant)
Abstract/Synopsis	Executive Summary
Introduction	Introduction
Body	Body
Methodology	Results
Results	Discussion
Discussion	Recommendations (if relevant)
Recommendations (if relevant)	Conclusions
Conclusions	Reference List/Endnotes

Reference List/Endnotes (depending on the referencing system recommended)
Appendices

(depending on the referencing system recommended)
Appendices

The report form is rather strict, in both presentation and the systematic approach to how the argument is developed, in comparison with other written documents such as an essay. As reports draw on facts and details from other sources make sure you cite these sources appropriately.

✓ CHECKLIST: WRITTEN REPORTS

❑ Is a presentable cover page included?

❑ Are the ideas easy and clear to follow?

❑ Is the synopsis/executive summary clear and succinct?

❑ Does the introduction state the focus of the research clearly?

❑ Have all the main points been included?

❑ Have they been supported adequately?

❑ Is a list of tables/figures included?

❑ Does the conclusions section bring the main ideas together clearly?

❑ Are all the references cited according to the conventions of the system nominated by the lecturer?

❏ Do the headings reflect what is included in each section?

❏ Are the sections in the correct order?

❏ Are all the figures/tables included?

❏ Are all the figures/tables illustrated clearly?

❏ Is a brief description of each table/figure included?

❏ Are tables/figures numbered appropriately?

❏ Are all the appendices included?

❏ Is the references list included?

❏ Has the report been double-spaced (if required)?

9

Referencing

Referencing is a crucial part of academic study. It demonstrates that you are aware of the arguments involved in an issue and can add to them through your own ideas. During the course of your studies you will come across information from a variety of sources, both print and online. It is important to acknowledge the sources you have used to prepare a task or assignment by following referencing rules or conventions. Most disciplines require you to follow a particular referencing system; your department will inform you of the appropriate system and may even provide a handout to follow. This chapter explains how to cite various sources of information, both print and electronic based, following the conventions of the three main referencing systems: the Harvard Referencing System (Intext or Author-Date System), the Footnote/Endnote System (or Oxford System) and the American Psychological Association (APA) System. It goes over the conventions of each system in regard to citing print and electronic sources and shows you how to write up a bibliography or references list.

THE IMPORTANCE OF REFERENCING

Becoming familiar with the authorities and the various arguments important in your area of study is an essential part of entering into academic discourse. You will be expected to read widely and to have a general understanding of the discipline. Also, you should demonstrate your knowledge by drawing on the views of authorities during discussions and in your assignments. Your approach should be a critical one, in which you draw upon your reading to support your argument, present an opposing view or to outline a general review of the topic. When you present a critical argument which draws on the views and research of scholars, you are entering into **academic discourse**.

The thing to remember is that whenever you quote or use information from another source, this source must be acknowledged. Failing to acknowledge another person's ideas or research findings is known as **plagiarism** and is a serious matter in an institution whose main commodity is ideas.

> **PLAGIARISM**
>
> Plagiarism entails the failure to acknowledge a source. This can occur when a student passes off someone else's argument, ideas or results as his/her own. It is a serious matter, along the same lines as stealing. Penalties may include having to resubmit an assignment, automatic failing of an assignment or course, a fine or, in some cases, being dismissed from the institution.

A REFERENCE

A full reference (citation) includes the source's author, publication date, title of the text, publisher and place published. Reviewing your course textbooks will give you an idea of how an author cites other sources in a reference. This is done as a matter of acknowledgment. It is also helpful to anyone who would like to investigate a topic more closely. The most important thing is to be *consistent* in your use of italics, punctuation and inclusion of details.

An example of a full reference for a book:

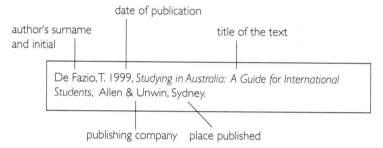

date of publication

author's surname
and initial

title of the text

De Fazio, T. 1999, *Studying in Australia: A Guide for International Students*, Allen & Unwin, Sydney.

publishing company   place published

An example of a full reference for a journal:

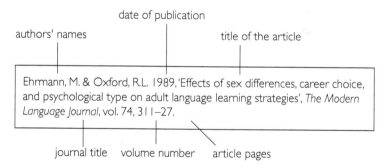

date of publication

authors' names

title of the article

Ehrmann, M. & Oxford, R.L. 1989, 'Effects of sex differences, career choice, and psychological type on adult language learning strategies', *The Modern Language Journal*, vol. 74, 311–27.

journal title   volume number   article pages

THE HARVARD REFERENCING SYSTEM

Under the conventions of the Harvard Referencing System (or Author/Date System) references are made in the body of the text and the full citation details given in the bibliography or references list. The name of the author appears first, followed by the year of publication, a comma and then the precise page reference.

> Germov (1996, p.94) states that 'referencing can seem the most confusing aspect of essay writing. However, it is simply a technique that shows the reader where you got the information you used in your essay.'

Under the Harvard System, the **full citation** for a text in the reference list or bibliography appears as:

> Bell, C., Bowden, M. & Trott, A. 1997, *Implementing Flexible Learning: Aspects of Educational and Training Technology*, Kogan Page, London.

In the text a **general reference** to an argument is presented as:

> De Winton (1998) expounds that technology . . .

or

> The idea that technology is dramatically changing the way society approaches education is expounded by De Winton (1998).

In the case of a **direct reference** to an author's argument, the author's name is given, with the year and, if appropriate, page details included in brackets:

> De Winton postulates (1998, pp.35–6) that technology is a source of concern in regard to its effects on social aspects such as employment opportunities.

If a **general reference** is made to a work:

> There are some researchers (William 1998, Lu 1999) who disagree with De Winton (1998), maintaining that . . .

The same conventions apply when **referring to several authors**, that is, after the authors' surnames the dates of their work appear in brackets:

> Smith (1998), Tran (1999) and Marius (1997) suggest that . . .

Alternatively, you could list the authors and their dates in brackets, separating them with a semi-colon:

> The general proposition that education is undergoing certain value changes has been widely suggested (Smith 1998; Tran 1999; Marius 1997).

Sometimes an author has more than one work that is useful. **Referring to more than one work by an author** follows the same convention as for separate works, except they are set out chronologically (according to the date of publication):

> Research by Luca (1997, 1998, 2000) consistently demonstrates that . . .

Referring to a **journal article** follows the same pattern, listing the author's surname, date and page reference (if applicable):

> Bates (1997) theorises that . . .

The full citation would appear in the reference list or bibliography as:

> Bates, A.W. 1997, 'The impact of technological change on open and distance learning', *Distance Education*, vol. 18, no.1, pp.93–109.

Citing **articles in newspapers** follows the same pattern: the name of the newspaper, the date, section (if applicable) and the page:

Il Mondo (1 August 1999, p.A20) reported that . . .

When there is an **identifiable author** of a newspaper article the citation is the same as for a journal:

Luca, D. (1999, p.22) . . .

The full reference would appear as:

Luca, D. 1999, 'Active babies', *The Times Weekly*, 24 February, p.12.

Reference to **an author who has published several texts in one year** may sometimes occur. To distinguish between the works, letters of the alphabet are used, with a semi-colon to separate them. The references follow in order of the alphabet in the bibliography or reference list:

O'Malley (1999a; 1999b) reports that . . .

In the case of **two authors,** both names are given. Where the reference appears in brackets in the text you can use the symbol & instead of the word 'and' between the authors' names:

Preciso and Corretto (1997) indicate . . .

Recent research (Preciso & Corretto, 1997) indicates that . . .

When there are **three authors or more**, the in-text reference need only give the first author's name, followed by the Latin abbreviation et al., which indicates there are other authors. All of the authors' names appear in the bibliography or reference list in the order they appear on the title page of the document.

Luca et al. (1998, p.7) claim that . . .

You may find that you need to refer to **an author who appears in a text collated by an editor or another author.** The rules are the same: the author you quote appears in the in-text reference and the editor or other author details appear in the reference list or bibliography. Note that the abbreviation ed. is used for editor:

Grata (1998) states . . .

The full reference would appear as:

Grata, M. I. 1998, 'Tosca's pain' in *Great Operas,* L. Toscanini (ed.), Verdi Publishing, Verona.

On occasions you may need to refer to an **organisation** as the author of material. This is usually the case with reports and government documents. Here the organisation's name, or the abbreviation for it, is used in place of the author. If the abbreviation is commonly used, it can be used in the body of your assignment:

As indicated by DEET (1997) . . .

The organisation's full name must be outlined in the bibliography. The full reference, with the edition used clearly identified, would be:

Department of Education, Employment and Training, 1997. *Transition issues for first year university students,* AGPS, Canberra.

Referencing **government publications** is similar to other documents. The author is the government department or committee as detailed in the title of the document. The convention is similar to the pattern outlined so far:

Department of Multicultural Affairs (1999) figures show . . .

THE FOOTNOTE/ENDNOTE SYSTEM

This system (also referred to as the Oxford System) is characterised by having each in-text citation numbered sequentially. The corresponding full reference is inserted at the bottom of the page as a **footnote**, or in a list of **endnotes** at the end of the chapter or the assignment. It is important to remember that the references appear in the order that the works are mentioned in the main text. Your word processing program may format the number automatically in your assignment, or you can select the *superscript* function under *font*. (Alternatively, typing the number within the text in parentheses is acceptable.) Unlike the Harvard and APA systems, the author's first name or initial appears before the surname, followed by a comma and the title, which is italicised or underlined. The page number appears at the end of the citation.

> Germov (1996, p.94) states that 'referencing can seem the most confusing aspect of essay writing. However, it is simply a technique that shows the reader where you got the information you used in your essay.'[3]

The full reference would appear as a footnote or endnote as:

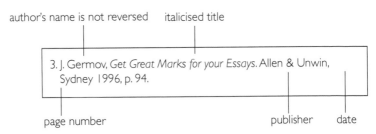

author's name is not reversed   italicised title

3. J. Germov, *Get Great Marks for your Essays*. Allen & Unwin, Sydney 1996, p. 94.

page number   publisher   date

Mentioning the author in the text is also indicated by citation number:

> De Winton[1] suggests that technology . . .

or

It has been suggested[1] that . . .

The citation appearing at the foot of the page or as an endnote would be:

1. L. De Winton, *Technological Times,* Cippo University Press, Reponds, 1998, pp.36–9.

When there are **three authors or more,** the in-text reference gives the first author only, followed by et al. to indicate that there are other authors.

Luca et al.[1] claims that . . .

All of the authors' names appear in the full citation in the order they appear on the title page of the document.

1. D. Luca, P. De Winton, S. Scema, *Culture and Society*, Gibili Press, Gosford, 1999.

When referring to **an author who appears in a text collated by an editor or another author,** that author appears in the in-text reference while the details of the editor (or other author) appear in the full citation. Remember that the abbreviation ed. is used for editor:

Grata[6] states . . .

The full reference appears as:

6. M. I. Grata, 'Tosca's pain' in *Great Operas,* L. Toscanini (ed.), Verdi Publishing, Verona, 1998.

When **referring to several authors** the authors' surnames are listed:

Smith[1], Tran[2] and Marius[3] suggest that . . .

The full references appear as:

1. A. Smith, *Technology and Society*, Cippo University Press, Responds 1998.
2. Y. Tran, *Flexible Learning Environments*, Peppe Press, Sillo, 1997.
3. M. Marius, *Student Needs and Learning Environments*, Pesce Press, Milo, 2001.

When **referring more than once to the same work by the same author**, the full citation is given for the first occurrence, and subsequent citations are represented by the Latin abbreviation ibid. This directs the reader to the full reference above:

1. D. Luca, 'Active babies', *The Times Weekly*, 24 February, 1999, pp. 12–16.
2. ibid., p.13.
3. ibid., p.16.

More than one reference to a resource that is not mentioned sequentially in the body of text is demonstrated by the Latin abbreviation *op.cit*. This abbreviation is preceded by the surname so that the reader can refer to the author and page details.

1. A. Smith, *Technology and Society*, Cippo University Press, Responds 1998.
2. Y. Tran, *Flexible Learning Environments*, Peppe Press, Sillo, 1997.
3. Smith, *op. cit.*, p.22.

Citations referring to **an author who has published several texts** are organised in a similar fashion. The references follow in chronological order. When differentiation between **two texts**

published in the same year by the same author needs to be made, the texts are indicated alphabetically:

Various studies by Luca[1] demonstrate that . . .

The full citation would appear as:

1. D. Luca, 'Male children', Paperino Books, Venice, 1996.
   D. Luca, 'Rearing sons', Paperino Books, Venice, 1999a.
   D. Luca, 'Active babies', *The Times Weekly*, 24 February, 1999b, pp.12–16.

A **reference to a journal article** contains similar information as well as volume and issue number. The article appears in quotation marks while the title of the journal appears in italics:

Bates suggests[4] that . . .

The full citation would appear as:

A. W. Bates, 'The impact of technological change on open and distance learning', *Distance Education*, vol. 18., no.1, 1997, pp.93–109.

Citing **articles in newspapers** follows a similar pattern:

Luca[5] reported that . . .

The full reference would appear as:

5. D. Luca, 'Active babies', *The Times Weekly*, 24 February, 1999, p.12.

When referring to an **organisation** as the author of material such as reports or government documents, the organisation's name is used in place of the author:

As indicated by DEET[16] . . .

The full reference, with the edition used clearly identified, would be:

16. Department of Education, Employment and Training, *Transition issues for first year university students,* AGPS, Canberra, 1997.

Figure 8.1 Abbreviations commonly used in referencing

edn	edition	vol./Vol.	volume
ed.	editor or edition	p.	page
eds	editors or editions	pp.	pages
et al.	(*et alii*) and others	Re	regarding
ibid.	(*ibidem*) in the same place	V	version
op. cit.	(*opere citato*) in the work cited already	no./No.	number

THE AMERICAN PSYCHOLOGICAL ASSOCIATION (APA) REFERENCING SYSTEM

The APA system is used mainly in the health sciences. It is similar to the Harvard System so be wary of confusing them. References are made in the body of the text just as in the Harvard System and the full citation details appear in the bibliography or references list. The in-text citations for general and direct references, as well as for several authors and for an author who has published several texts, are the same as under the Harvard system—this applies to any type of source, whether text, journal or electronic. This is an example of an in-text citation:

> Germov (1996, p.94) states that 'referencing can seem the most confusing aspect of essay writing. However, it is simply a technique that shows the reader where you got the information you used in your essay.'

The APA system is different when you look closely at the full citation for each type of source. The full citation for a **text** using the APA system would appear in the reference list or bibliography as:

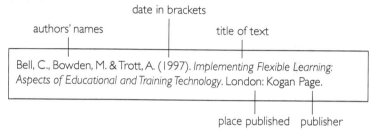

A citation for a **journal** would appear in the reference list or bibliography as:

> Bates, A.W. (1997). 'The impact of technological change on open and distance learning'. *Distance Education, 18(1)*, 93–109.

The full reference for **articles in newspapers** follows the same sort of citation pattern:

> Luca, D. (1999). 'Active babies'. *The Times Weekly*, 24 February, 12.

When referring to **an author who appears in a text collated by an editor or another author** the rules are the same: the author's name appears as the in-text reference and the editor or other author details appear in the reference list or bibliography.

> Grata (1998) states . . .

The full reference would appear as:

> Grata, M. I. (1998). 'Tosca's Pain' in *Great Operas*. L. Toscanini (ed.), Verona: Verdi Publishing.

A full reference when citing an **organisation** as the author appears as:

> Department of Education, Employment and Training (1997). *Transition issues for first year university students.* Canberra: AGPS.

REFERENCING ELECTRONIC SOURCES

Electronic sources such as the Web, CD-ROMs and e-mail are being used more frequently in academic research. Referencing conventions are still being consolidated by the International Organisation for Standardization and the American Psychological Association (APA). The following guide brings together the current conventions for electronic citations. Useful references, where you can check for later modifications, are included in Appendix 1.

Online sources

Citations for online sources follow a similar pattern to those already outlined. Wherever there is an identifiable author, his or her name is used as in citations for print material. Sometimes you need to scan the electronic material carefully to discover the author's name; in e-mails, for instance, the name may be found at the end of the page as an e-mail address. You may at times find only a nickname or *handle*, in which case you would use the handle as the author's details. The full date, that is, the day, month and year when the work was published, usually appears either at the beginning or at the end of a web page; on a commercial program it normally appears at the beginning. Where there are no date details the abbreviation 'n.d.' (no date) can be used (for example, Bianca, n.d.). Just as with any other source of information, the full title of the information must be detailed. It is important to add the type of document, such as [WWW document], to indicate that the material was found on the Web. It is quite easy to get the details of the Web address or URL (Uniform Resource Locator) incorrect, so take care to provide the precise elements. If a URL is longer than one line it is broken at a slash and continued on a second line. Remember too that a URL has no punctuation mark at the end. The date the work is accessed should also be included. Anyone who uses the online environment for a while will realise soon enough that sites are modified frequently; if this happens, the inclusion of the access date in the full citation will demonstrate that the site was viewed before the modifications were made.

Harvard Referencing System

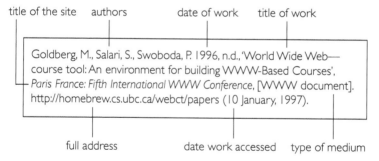

Footnote Referencing System:

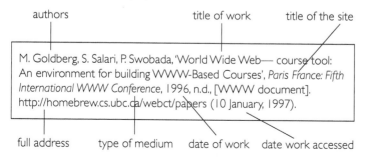

APA Referencing System

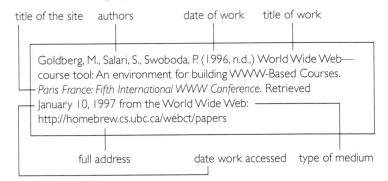

title of the site   authors   date of work   title of work

> Goldberg, M., Salari, S., Swoboda, P. (1996, n.d.,) World Wide Web—
> course tool: An environment for building WWW-Based Courses.
> *Paris France: Fifth International WWW Conference.* Retrieved
> January 10, 1997 from the World Wide Web:
> http://homebrew.cs.ubc.ca/webct/papers

full address   date work accessed   type of medium

Journals and newspaper articles on the Internet

Newspaper articles, academic and popular journal articles are now accessible electronically, either online or as part of a database. The full web address must be included if the document was retrieved online.

Harvard Referencing System

> White, F. 1999, 'Digital Diploma Mills: A Dissenting Voice', *First Monday*, Issue 4, N.7, [Online journal] http://www.firstmonday. org/issues/issue4_7/white/ (date accessed 12 August, 2000)

Footnote System

> 1. F. White, 'Digital Diploma Mills: A Dissenting Voice', *First Monday*, 1999, Issue 4, N.7, [Online journal] http://www.firstmonday.org/issues/issue4_7/white/ (date accessed 12 August, 2000)

APA Referencing System

> White, F. (1999). Digital Diploma Mills: A Dissenting Voice. *First Monday, 4(7).* Retrieved August 12, 2000 from the World Wide Web: http://www.firstmonday.org/issues/issue4_7/white/

Citing CD-ROM information

The great advantage of CD-ROMs is that they store enormous amounts of information. The way you cite this material follows a similar pattern for each of the reference systems. The details include the author's name, the date, the title of the article, the name of the CD-ROM, the version (if applicable), identification of the medium, and the name of the publishing company.

Harvard Referencing System

> Tardis, M. (2001) 'Zoppicare Zoppicas,' *Dante's Inferno Revisited*, V. 2 [CDROM] Literaturas Corporation.

Footnote Referencing System

> 1. M. Tardis, 'Zoppicare Zoppicas,' *Dante's Inferno Revisited*, V. 2 [CDROM] Literaturas Corporation, 2001.

APA Referencing System

> Tardis, M. (2001). Zoppicare Zoppicas. *Dante's Inferno Revisited*, *V. 2*. From CD-ROM Literaturas Corporation.

Citing information from discussion lists

As part of your research-gathering process you may find yourself in the situation of citing information gained from a **discussion list**. The conventions for these also vary.

Harvard Referencing System

> Coco, L. 1 March, 1998. 'The pressure is on'. *Parenting and Psychology*, [Online] Available from: Parentliest@psychvu.lv.au (11 April, 1998).

Footnote Referencing System

> 1. L. Coco, 'The pressure is on'. *Parenting and Psychology*, 1998, 1 March, [Online] Available from: Parentliest@psychvu.lv.au (11 April, 1998).

APA Referencing System

> Coco, L. (1998, March 1). The pressure is on. Formal discussion initiation. *Parenting and Psychology.* Retrieved April 11, 1998 from the listserv: Parentliest@psychvu.lv.au

Citing e-mails

Referencing conventions also apply when citing **personal e-mails.** As part of your study activities you may be in e-mail contact with other professionals, lecturers, authors or other authorities on a subject. This information may be useful to your studies and you may wish to draw upon it; in so doing, it must be acknowledged.

Harvard Referencing System

> Coco, L. (cocol@cuoresmama.com.vs), 2 September, 2000, Re: *The Beautiful Life* (Film), E-mail to E. Vici (vicie@sempremail.com.vs).

Footnote Referencing System

> 1. L. Coco (cocol@cuoresmama.com.vs), Re: *The Beautiful Life* (Film). E-mail to E. Vici (vicie@sempremail.com.vs). 2 September, 2000.

APA Referencing System

The *Electronic Reference Formats* (2000), published by the APA, recommends that e-mail communication be cited as personal messages and not included as a reference. Personal communication can be referred to in the following way:

> L. Coco (personal communication, March 8, 2000) outlined what he views to be the major themes of *The Beautiful Life*.

THE BIBLIOGRAPHY OR REFERENCES LIST

Which should it be?

It is important to clarify with your lecturer whether a reference list or a bibliography should be part of your assignment. While the manner in which material is detailed is the same for both, the reference list gives only the sources cited in the body of your written assignment. A bibliography is an extended list that includes all the relevant sources used in preparing the assignment, even though you may not have cited them specifically.

Presentation

The presentation details of a reference list or bibliography depend on the referencing system adopted for the body of the text. The main feature is that the citations are presented in alphabetical order according to the author's surname. Convention dictates that the second and subsequent lines of a citation are indented to highlight this order. References should always be consistently set out and punctuated according to the referencing system you use; the correct positioning of commas and full stops is important, even though this point may seem trivial. Ensure that each of the texts is cited according to the original language used, particularly if dealing with foreign languages. Too often students make the error of writing up each reference in a different way. Consistency is important. One more point: if a lecturer asks that texts, journals and electronic sources be separated into different sections, the same conventions apply.

If you use the footnote/endnote system, there is probably no need to attach a reference list or bibliography unless your lecturer asks for it specifically, but it would be worth checking. If it is required, the format is exactly the same as for the footnotes/endnotes themselves, except that the surname appears before the initials so that the alphabetical order is highlighted and page numbers are not required except in the case of journal articles. Although these are only minor differences it is important not to get confused—consistency is important.

Harvard Referencing System

Figure 9.2 is an example of a bibliography or reference list according to the Harvard Referencing System.

Figure 9.2 Bibliography/reference list under Harvard Referencing System

Australian Government Publishing Service 1994, *Style Manual: for Authors, Editors and Printers*, 5th edn. AGPS, Canberra.

Bell, C., Bowden, M. & Trott, A. 1997, *Implementing Flexible Learning: Aspects of Educational and Training Technology*, Kogan Page, London.

De Fazio, T. 1999, *Studying in Australia: A Guide for International Students*, Allen & Unwin, Sydney.

Ehrmann, M. & Oxford, R. L. 1989, 'Effects of sex differences, career choice, and psychological type on adult language learning strategies', *The Modern Language Journal*, vol. 74, pp. 311–27.

Luca, D. 1999, 'Active babies', *The Times Weekly*, 24 February, p. 12.

Wajcman, J. 1994, 'Technological a/genders: technology, culture and class' in *Framing Technology: Society, Choice and Change*, L. Green & R. Guinery (eds), Allen & Unwin, Sydney.

The Footnote/Endnote System

The bibliography would be identical to the footnote or endnote citations already outlined in this chapter. The only difference is that the author's surname is put at the beginning of the reference in order to arrange the references alphabetically. Figure 9.3 gives an example.

Figure 9.3 Bibliography under Footnote/Endnote System

Bates, A. W. 'The impact of technological change on open and distance learning', *Distance Education*. vol. 18. no.1, 1997, pp.93–109.

Department of Education, Employment and Training. *Transition issues for first year university students*. AGPS, Canberra, 1997.

De Winton, L. *Technological Times*. Cippo University Press, Reponds, 1998, pp.36–9.

Grata, M. I. 'Tosca's pain' in *Great Operas*. L. Toscanini (ed.), Verdi Publishing, Verona, 1998.

Luca, D. *Rearing Sons*. Paperino Books, Venice, 1999a.

Luca, D. 'Active babies', *The Times Weekly*. 24 February, 1999b, pp.12–16.

Luca, D., De Winton, P., Scema, S. *Culture and Society*. Gibili Press, Gosford, 1999.

Smith, A. *Technology and Society*. Cippo University Press, Reponds, 1998.

Tran, Y. *Flexible Learning Environments*. Peppe Press, Sillo, 1997.

APA Referencing System

Figure 9.4 is an example of a bibliography or reference list according to the APA Referencing System.

Figure 9.4 Bibliography/reference list under APA System

Australian Government Publishing Service. (1994). *Style Manual: for Authors, Editors and Printers*, 5th edn. Canberra: AGPS.

Bell, C., Bowden, M. & Trott, A. (1997). *Implementing Flexible Learning: Aspects of Educational and Training Technology*. London: Kogan Page.

De Fazio, T. (1999). *Studying in Australia: A Guide for International Students*. Sydney: Allen & Unwin.

Ehrmann, M. & Oxford, R. L. (1989). Effects of sex differences, career choice, and psychological type on adult language learning strategies. *The Modern Language Journal, 74*, 311–27.

Luca, D. (1999). Active babies. *The Times Weekly*, 24 February, 12.

Wajcman, J. (1994). Technological a/genders: technology, culture and class in *Framing Technology: Society, Choice and Change*. L. Green & R. Guinery (eds). Sydney: Allen & Unwin.

It is important to adhere to the conventions of the referencing system used in your discipline. Ensure that all the details are included, that punctuation is accurate and that references are presented according to the guidelines set out in this chapter. It may seem somewhat tedious, but your lecturers will look carefully at how well you handle referencing.

✓ CHECKLIST: REFERENCING

❑ The referencing system used is the one recommended by your lecturer.

❑ Only one style of referencing has been used and there is no jumping between different styles.

❑ Details of sources have been copied correctly.

❑ The edition is clearly identified.

❑ The text is cited according to the original language.

❑ Each footnote (if used) is separated by a double line.

❑ Citations for journal references include volume and issue number, if applicable.

❑ References for electronic sources detail the type of medium.

❑ References for websites include the date accessed.

❑ The sources of your quotes appear in the references list or bibliography.

❑ Resource details in the bibliography or references list appear in alphabetical order according to author surnames.

❑ The second and subsequent lines of a reference in the bibliography or reference list are indented.

❑ Alphabetical notes distinguish two publications in one year by the same author (e.g. 1996a and 1996b).

❑ Under the footnote system, the sources are numbered in the order they appear in the text (not appropriate in the bibliography or references list).

10

Exams

Exam times are often times of nervousness or even stress, but there are advantages to taking them. Exams mean that your assessment is undertaken in a short period rather than spread over weeks. You generally need to present much less information than if you had to prepare a series of written assignments and you do not have to be as concerned over presentation issues as you are with written assignments.

Your course outline should explain how much of your assessment will be based on exams and what sort of exams you should expect. Knowing this will allow you to choose a study strategy that makes exam preparation an efficient and stress-free process. There are different types of exams: standard exams, taken in a room or hall; open-book exams, taken either in an exam room or at home, in which you are allowed to refer to certain texts; and take-home exams, for which you are given a night or a number of days to complete the exam. Each has time restrictions, each can be stressful if not prepared for adequately. This chapter looks at strategies for preparing for exams and strategies for sitting them.

REVISING

You may find that some revision time is built into your course, with a period of lecturer-led revision and one of self-directed revision, usually a week or two just before the exams. Some lecturers hold sessions on the marking schedule of exam questions. This is quite useful, because it explains what examiners look for and how they come to decide on an answer's validity. The lecturer may detail how many and what type of questions will be included, whether the format will differ from past exams and even the range of topics that will be covered. If such a session is not scheduled, you may choose to request one.

You will quickly discover that revising is not just a matter of rereading notes and highlighting main points with coloured pens. To prepare effectively for an exam you need to do more than passive revision just beforehand. Effective revision takes place at the end of every week or two and at the end of every topic studied during the year (or semester) so that you are constantly thinking about your work and are in a position to see how issues are evolving. Frequent revising forces you to *think* about the topic and the course as you proceed. This means that not only will your participation in the course be enhanced, but your exam preparation will also be more effective—you will not have to revise the whole course in the week before the exams. Gaining an overview of the important issues as you go through the course will give you a fair idea of the sort of exam questions you might encounter. The student who claims not to have studied all year, and just crammed during the week before the exam, is not so rare, but the student who actually passes this way really is rare.

Review your notes frequently to refresh your memory. Also keep note of how much time was devoted to covering each topic in a subject, and how much information was covered—this will indicate whether the topic is likely to appear on the exam. Of course, you need to prepare more topics than those suggested by this tactic. Some exams give you a choice of topics, others do not, so you need to be thorough in your preparation.

Arrange your notes to form a helpful record of the topics you need to cover. You might find visuals and flowcharts helpful in revision, using them to summarise or display cause and effect; tables can help you make comparisons; mindmaps are helpful when analysing links or brainstorming aspects of an issue. Such visuals and your notes are of great assistance in open-book or take-home exams and help make the revision process before other exams less stressful. Reread your notes in an active way, almost as if you were engaged in finding the information for the first time. Past exam questions, or making up your own questions, might also guide your revision.

Another effective approach to revision, particularly for those who prefer an interpersonal study style, is to form a study group, where you revise in a collaborative sense, going over important issues and readings, work on past exam questions together, compare notes on possible answers or review each other's responses.

PAST EXAM PAPERS

A useful way to practise for exams is to work through past exams (drawing on the questions that cover the topics covered in your course) under simulated exam conditions. This not only refreshes the memory but also provides the opportunity to practise working under strict time conditions and working intensively. Look at previous exam papers in terms of the sort of questions asked, the format of the paper, any recurring question and the style of answer required—essay, short answer, multiple choice. Also check on time limits given to certain question types, the marks allocated to various questions, the sort of instructions given and whether there are optional questions. Formats can change from year to year, however, so you might ask your lecturer whether there are differences this year. Even if there are changes, past exams are useful practise tools. They may be available from your lecturer or kept in the library.

You might find that you cannot complete the first two or three practise exams in the time allowed. If this happens, take a deep breath and be thankful you have given yourself time to practise getting faster! Past exams are also useful in directing discussion in a study group. Brainstorming on what a question is asking from you, and what should be covered in the answer, can be invaluable in terms of the different perspectives you gain. Another way to make use of past exams is to use the questions and your answers as the basis for a discussion with your lecturer. If there are no past exam papers available for practise, make up your own.

ORGANISING A REVISION SCHEDULE

Formulate your revision schedule as a strategy that will keep you focused on studying effectively rather than falling into one of the time-wasting traps that can tempt you before the exams. Start by reviewing the course exam timetable and prioritising the topics you need to cover, allocating a period of time to each subject and each particular topic. Allocate the first day or two to going over notes, the rest of the time to practise exams. Include sufficient short breaks to keep you from becoming overtired, over-anxious and ineffective. Build in a few rewards to keep your motivation levels and health up—for instance, a short walk, a relaxing bath or a quiet coffee and reading the paper at your favourite coffee shop. If your adrenalin levels are high you may need to include some intensive exercise time. Figure 10.1 outlines an example exam preparation schedule. Figure 10.2 details some time-wasting traps and strategies for avoiding them.

Figure 10.1 Exam preparation schedule

Time	Monday–Tuesday	Wednesday	Thursday	Friday (Study leave)	Saturday	Sunday
8.00–9.00	Reading/travel (Management notes)	Reading/travel (Economics notes)	Reading/travel (Economics notes)	Reading (Economics notes)	Reading (Economics notes)	Reading (Management notes)
9.00–5.30	Work	Work 5pm Gym	Work	Coffee break (11.00–11.30) Past exam paper: Economics (11.30–1.30) Lunch (1.30–2.30) Past exam paper: Economics (2.30–5.30)	Gym (11.00–12.30) Lunch (12.30–1.30) Read over Management notes (1.30–5.00) Break	Past exam paper: Management (9.00–12.30) Lunch and short walk (12.30–1.30) Study Group: Management Go over notes and past exam paper (1.30–6.00)
5.30–6.30	Travel home/read over notes Dinner	Travel home Dinner	Travel Dinner	Dinner	Read over Management notes	Dinner and evening social activities
6.30–7.00	Family/free time	Family time	Study Group: Economics Go over notes and past exam papers	Family time	Dinner and evening social activities	
7.00–10.00	Past exam paper: Management	Read over Economics notes (9.00–10.00)		Read over Economics notes (9.00–10.00)		

At the risk of sounding like your mother, eat well and get enough sleep! Nutritious food will ensure that you feel good and perform well. The habit of working well into the night will only fatigue you; you are much better off getting a good night's sleep so that you start the next day feeling refreshed.

Figure 10.2 Strategies for avoiding time-wasting traps

Traps	Strategies
• Procrastinating by putting non-study activities first or concentrating on one study task and avoiding others.	• Stop and recognise what you are doing. • Write up a realistic study schedule that will help you focus your attention. • Slot in rewards at the end of each study task (a short walk, a relaxing bath). • Prioritise tasks. Write them up and tick each one off as it is completed.
• Feeling anxious and studying sporadically.	• Think about why you are anxious and encourage yourself to study, which will lessen anxiety during the exam itself. • Formulate a revision schedule to keep yourself on track. • Practise deep breathing whenever you find anxiety building up.
• 'Imitation studying'—doing things that seem to be study	• Write up a prioritised list of study activities and allot a time

tasks but are ineffective, such as endlessly rewriting notes.	to each one to help focus your energies.
• Overstudying by spending too much time poring over notes, for instance, or doing past exams one after another, until you feel bombarded and overloaded with information.	• Work out a list of study tasks according to what you need to achieve, then carry them out in a methodical way, thinking about each one; reread the sections on focusing and critical thinking, reading, writing and listening (pp. 21, 25–7, 71, 86–7, 53). • Take breaks and rest.
• Studying without taking anything in.	• Vary study tasks so that you do not become bored. • Schedule breaks and eat well. • Focus on one study task at a time, considering the six inquiry questions. • Form a study group or find someone to listen while you go over your notes; this will start you thinking critically.

ESSAYS IN EXAMS

You may be asked to take an exam that includes writing an essay, either in the exam hall or as part of a take-home exam. The concepts that apply to writing essays as assignments also apply to writing essays in exams (following a basic structure and developing a line of critical argument), but in a time-pressured situation. The positive aspect is that you will normally have had some practise in writing essays during the year. The negative side is that there is no time for redrafting so your first draft is also your final draft and therefore needs to be at least reasonable. The trick is to plan your essay answer to avoid making, as far as is possible under stressful conditions, common mistakes such as digressing, not answering the question, being verbose and writing around the topic without actually answering the question. Remember your critical thinking, consider what the question is asking and jot down your stance. Then write down your main ideas in point form with supporting evidence or examples under each one. You will not be required to use references in as systematic or detailed a manner as you would in non-exam conditions, but it does help to include main ideas from your readings to support your argument—for example, 'Isabella (2001) holds that . . . while Gianni (2000) theorises that . . .' No reference list or bibliography is required when you do a paper in the exam hall, but check what is required for take-home exams. If a reference list is necessary, your record of sources will be a valuable asset (*see* Recording your sources, pp. 82–3).

TAKE-HOME EXAMS

Revise for these exams as you would for any other, organising your notes carefully beforehand so that you do not have to waste time looking up details. It is helpful to draw up a type of contents list of topics, arguments or examples, with related references and page numbers. Themes or aspects can be indicated by colour-coded Post-it® notes inserted in texts. Your resources reference list and material will be much more useful to you if it is neatly organised and accessible in a folder. Relevant practise exam notes can be organised in your folder too. Any memory-jogging posters and mindmaps that you have arranged around your study may also be useful. Have reference material such as dictionaries or manuals on hand.

SHORT-ANSWER QUESTIONS

Some exams are based entirely or in part on short-answer questions. Your answers need to be very specific as there is normally a strict word limit. Planning the answer by jotting down a few points will help keep you focused on answering the question and avoiding digression. Keep to the rules of good writing: have a clear topic sentence in each paragraph so that the main idea stands out from the supporting statements; use connecting statements between paragraphs to guide reader focus; and include short statements as the introduction and conclusion to assist in framing the answer.

MULTIPLE-CHOICE EXAMS

Some exams are made up of multiple-choice questions, which may seem easy at first glance but can prove rather tricky. Each statement or question has a number of possible answers; the differences between the answers can lie in the meaning of a word, the grammatical structure or even the punctuation. Read each word in each possible answer a number of times so that you are quite sure of the meaning. Normally there is one answer that is clearly wrong and two or three answers that are quite close in meaning and might possibly be correct. Break each answer into chunks and consider the wording carefully, checking, for instance, for significant words such as: 'always', 'never', 'frequently', 'very'. If you are unsure, mark the one you think is probably correct and put an asterisk next to it in case you have time to come back to it later. An answer based on a calculated decision is better than no answer.

GOLDEN RULES FOR SITTING EXAMS

- Know in advance where and when each exam is scheduled; do not arrive late.
- Ensure you have all your materials ready the night before: pens, ruler, calculator, student card, etc.

- On exam day, wear something light and bring along a jumper; exam halls are notoriously either hot or cold.
- Check the back of the exam paper in case it is printed on both sides.
- Read the exam questions carefully during reading time to ensure you understand the requirements. Take careful note of instruction words. Consider the wording so that you end up answering the question.
- Read (and reread) *all* the questions before deciding which questions you might choose to do where a choice is given. Check to see how many questions you need to answer.
- Answer the question rather than writing down everything you remember on the topic. A fatal error is to lose the point of the question amongst the knowledge you have gained. Get to the point quickly.
- Ignore the people around you in the exam room and focus on the task.
- Plan your answers, particularly if you have to write short answers or essays.
- When given a choice of questions, avoid planning potential answers to all of them—you will undoubtedly run out of time if you do this.
- If you are unsure of an answer make a calculated guess. You may have a hunch which is worth acting on; sometimes you can work out an answer by going through the logic of the question. There is nothing to lose so a guess is better than nothing.
- Check the mark value of the questions and consider how you might allocate your time. For instance, it would be wiser to allocate more time to a question worth 30 points than to a question worth 5.
- If time runs out and you cannot complete a short answer or essay question, jot down clear notes or refer the examiner to an attached plan so the examiner can see what you would

have written. Partial points are better than none.

- Leave some time for proofreading your answers. Do this carefully, as writing under stress can sometimes lead to costly errors.
- Keep your handwriting legible; don't let it deteriorate under the stress. A brilliant answer is no use if the examiner cannot read it.
- If you get nervous, try your focusing exercises.

COPING WITH NERVES

A degree of anxiety or nervousness in an exam situation is quite natural and can often be used to your advantage. The extra adrenalin going through your body can give you a heightened sense of awareness and assist in performing well over a period of two or three hours. Too much tension, too much adrenalin, however, can sometimes make your mind go blank over a particular question. If this happens, try deep breathing and relaxing your shoulder and neck muscles, and then go on. Sometimes closing your eyes and deep breathing will help you block out your environment and allow your anxiety to subside. If you are still getting nowhere, just leave the question and go on to the next one. Keeping up the momentum of writing and thinking will make it easier to return to the tension-inducing question. If you are really stuck, go back to the six inquiry questions (who, what, where, why, when, how).

GETTING FEEDBACK

When the exams are over your natural inclination will probably be to take time out to relax—and deservedly so. Before you switch off completely, however, it would be helpful to ask your lecturers for feedback on your answers. Many will be quite willing to go through the exam questions, discussing where your answers demonstrate understanding or need improvement, information which will stand you in good stead for the future.

Exams can prove to be a rather anxious time but thorough preparation will give you the confidence needed to tackle them successfully. Develop some strategies for preparing and taking exams, and use exams as an opportunity to gain feedback on your progress and your understanding. This feedback will help direct your knowledge-building and facilitate your performance in further assessment tasks.

> **There is no such thing as a great talent without great willpower.**
>
> Honoré de Balzac

11

Research projects and theses

As part of your studies you may be asked to undertake a research project. Certainly at postgraduate level some sort of major project, dissertation or thesis is usually a requirement. A research project allows you to investigate a particular area of interest and perhaps contribute a different perspective, method or theory to the discipline. Thus it provides a way of contributing to academic discourse. This chapter outlines what is involved in preparing a research project along with a discussion of aspects relating to postgraduate studies in particular.

SURVIVING POSTGRADUATE STUDIES

Postgraduate studies differ from undergraduate studies in both practical and inherent features. Practical considerations include completion time, method of delivery and scheduling of classes. Inherent features of a course include course content, intensiveness of the pace, reading and writing demands, research requirements and assessment issues. Postgraduate studies are meant to be not only an exercise in the development of practical skills in a discipline, but also an experience which leads a student to develop higher-order thinking skills, knowledge levels, creativity and 'learning how to learn' strategies.

Postgraduate study modes are generally research based or coursework based, or a combination of the two. It is important to select the mode that suits your situation. Consider the amount of time and energy involved in the course: what it would mean each week to fulfil its requirements; the level of application involved (some Masters courses based on coursework may not be as demanding as those based on research); the sort of skills and knowledge you wish to achieve as an outcome; the vocational benefits, and how the course may fit into plans for future study. You may, for instance, convert from a postgraduate diploma to a Masters by coursework more easily than to a Masters by research, or you may be more likely to be considered for a PhD scholarship if you have undertaken a Masters by research. Explore the modes, think carefully about your objectives and talk to lecturers and colleagues before making a decision.

Make contact with the appropriate postgraduate association. This association can provide a lot of useful material and guidance—information on study skills support, seminars and workshops on aspects of postgraduate study, access to computer facilities, setting up an e-mail account, access to desk space, library information sessions, binding and copying services, scholarships and manuals on postgraduate studies at your particular institution. These manuals detail obligations on the part of both the research supervisor and the student. Most postgraduate associations also provide a handy fortnightly e-mail newsletter which lists events, services and scholarship information for postgraduate students. Opportunities to meet other postgraduate students are often organised as well, providing invaluable forums for discussing study and other issues. If you are a distance learning student you may ask to be linked up with other postgraduate students, particularly others studying in your discipline area. E-mail, chat and discussion lists can be valuable for communication with your peers and lecturers.

Scholarships, grants and bursaries can ease the financial pressure. There are usually a number of these on offer to post-graduate students, both locally and overseas. You need to check on closing dates for submission of documents; your institution and/or your department will have current information.

UNDERTAKING A RESEARCH PROJECT

Undertaking a research project generally involves thirteen steps that you need to plan carefully. They are summarised in Figure 11.1. Each stage will keep you busy note-taking, drafting and reading. The literature search never really ends with Step 7, however—it is a continuous process, particularly for research Masters and PhD students who are undertaking studies over an extended period. Aspects to keep in mind when planning and writing up your study include:

- the relevance of the information you use as a basis for the project;
- the applicability of the information (is it current?);
- the purpose or objective of the research project;
- your writing style;
- methodological aspects; and
- ethical considerations, especially when collecting data.

Figure 11.1 Thirteen steps to successful research study

1. Investigate the area in which you are interested by reading current publications. What is being said on the matter, and what is *not* being said? Your research question is likely to come out of your perspective on what is not being said.

2. Talk to lecturers, colleagues or other interested people about the topic and your ideas on how to tackle it.
3. Identify a general question.
4. If applicable, consult with prospective supervisors. Your choice of supervisor may dictate your choice of institution.
5. Write up a brief research proposal to be submitted with your candidature application.
6. Plan your research project, including a timeline, and submit it to your lecturer/supervisor for comment.
7. Do a literature search.
8. Refine and define your research question.
9. Investigate and select an appropriate research method.
10. Collect data.
11. Interpret data.
12. Write up the study.
13. Submit your project.

Identifying your research question

Step 8, refining and defining your research question, is most important. You are only able to do this effectively when you have got a real sense of the topic. Whether you are investigating arguments, methods, approaches, theories or models, you need to critically investigate what has already been presented to enable you to present your own perspective on it and thus bring something of value to the discussion: a new theory, model or approach. Explore current research to identify any 'holes', faults or perspectives that require attention; this is particularly important if you are undertaking a major research project or thesis as part of postgraduate studies. Next, ask yourself if you have chosen a topic that is manageable and is of real interest to you. Consider the timeframe, your energy levels and course objectives; you may have so much on your plate that it would be wiser not to write that PhD level thesis and to take on a Masters thesis instead. If you find that you

are so taken with your research topic that you are intent on undertaking it, discuss the option of being considered for PhD studies
with your supervisor. At whatever level you approach it, it is
important to choose a topic in which you are interested, one that
keeps nagging at you for attention, which will give you a better
chance of sustaining your motivation levels.

Once you have identified what you want to investigate, write
it down in one or two lines. Not that easy really! To make this
easier, think of having to explain your research topic to a person
outside your discipline.

TIME MANAGEMENT AND RESEARCH

Time-management skills are vital to postgraduate studies, especially when conducting research. Spending too much time on
one section of the research, or on other duties, can leave you with
inadequate time for the rest.

Even if your institution does not require you to present a
timeline, it is a good idea to plot out a realistic one for your own
benefit. Keep it in sight of your desk. Ask your lecturer or supervisor to check whether it appears practical. Stages that may need
to be allowed for in your time plan include:

- Literature review
- Full research proposal
- Data collection
- Data analysis
- Drafting
- Final writing up of project

FEELING ALONE

One of the problems most commonly faced by part-time postgraduate students is feeling isolated and alone. You will need to

develop a keen sense of yourself as an independent and self-motivated learner. Research-based part-time studies may require so much self-directed study that contact with staff and other students can become infrequent, and you need to be mentally prepared for this. Most universities have a good workshop program that allows you to meet others who are in the same situation and keen to exchange ideas or have coffee. The post-graduate associations at many universities hold social events as well as workshops. Directing your own line of study may also involve discussions with colleagues, people in the community and/or business organisations, academics in your own institution or outside whose ideas and publications are of interest.

Becoming too focused on your studies, however, can detract from your inspiration and motivation. You can end up feeling low, producing poor quality work and harming relations with your family and friends. Give yourself a little reward each time you meet a study goal. Think of study in the same way as work so that you don't allow yourself to become burnt out.

THE RESEARCH PROJECT

The literature search

Doing a literature search means that you investigate and document what has already been researched and discussed in your field of interest. It is a necessary part of the groundwork for your own research. You need to analyse where your topic sits in relation to other research in the area: perhaps your line of investigation is contrary to previous investigation, or it may approach the question from a perspective which brings different results.

A word of caution: at some time during your literature search you will feel overwhelmed, both by the amount of material and the directions in which it seems to be pulling you. While it is important to acknowledge these directions and even to investigate some of them, it is more important to keep focused on the nucleus of your own interest; you may occasionally have to reorient yourself. Your lecturer or supervisor can help here but you need to develop your own sense of focus.

The search will mean a lot of reading and a lot of time spent in the library. Using the library's electronic research facilities will make the whole process a lot less daunting. To make library work more productive, think about these questions:

- What are the key words that will help in finding relevant material?
- How far back do you intend to go? Are you interested only in recently published works?
- Who are the gurus in the field? What are their arguments? What have they written?
- What are the important works you must read?
- What types of materials may be of assistance? Will journals, theses, government reports and lab reports be relevant?

At some point during your search you will begin writing your literature review, which is a discussion of the reading you have undertaken of contemporary and important works relating to your argument. This section demonstrates that you are aware of the arguments in your area and allows you to set the scene for your research topic. It permits the reader to follow the issues that are central to your project and to understand the basis of your argument.

Methodology

The research method you select depends on your field of study and your research question. As a Masters or Doctorate level student you will need to take the initiative in exploring different approaches and discussing the merits of each with your supervisor who will help you identify the most appropriate method.

In the methodology section you need to rationalise three factors: your choice of sample group, how you will gather the data (and the rationale for choosing that method), and how you will handle the data and extract meaningful information from it. Ask your lecturer to recommend texts that will help in designing your research method.

Collecting and interpreting research data

This is a rather lengthy stage where planning ahead can save time and effort. Focus on how you will collect your data and consider what is actually required to answer your question. (It is not unusual for students to find they have collected interesting but completely irrelevant data, and to have to start all over again.) Your supervisor should help you here. Check that you can access the data you require; some data may be confidential information or you may need to use services which require special permission. Sometimes such data will be worth the extra effort, sometimes not. As you may only get one shot at collecting data, make sure you have all the information and equipment you need ready (and working)—copies of permission letters, interview schedules, lab equipment and so on.

The next stage is to explain how the data answers your question. You may set out tables of findings and point out what each set of data demonstrates. Use this section to highlight any significant and interesting aspects that have arisen from your data.

Writing it up

Finally, it is time to write your research up. Start with a writing plan which sets out the main headings and subheadings to lessen the likelihood of digressing or omitting important information. Assigning a word limit to each section also helps. Be prepared to do a number of drafts and probably to slave over expression as you aim for clarity and logic. It might help to think about the reader as someone with no background in the area whom you are taking through the discussion systematically. This helps pinpoint areas that may need explanation or clarification. Headings and subheadings are valuable both as markers and for cross-referencing. Your supervisor may recommend good theses in your field that you can read which may help you settle on appropriate writing strategies.

Different departments, faculties and institutions may have particular requirements for the presentation of the project. These may cover:

• Length (number of words)
• Presentation of figures/tables, etc.
• Presentation of appendices
• Size of margins
• Binding
• Number of copies
• Who the copies are submitted to
• Forms to be presented with the submission

Last but not least, be prepared to stop at some point and cut the 'umbilical cord' that connects you to the project. It is not uncommon to feel that the 'final draft' remains an illusion—but it is important to stop when you have done all that is reasonable and get on with your life while you await the results.

EXAMINATION

The examination of Masters and PhD level theses is usually undertaken by two examiners (not including your supervisor); usually one or both will be external to the university with some expertise in your area. Your patience might be tested as it may be eight weeks or more before you get the report. You may be asked to rewrite certain parts in response to comments made by the examiners. This is part of the process and quite common. Try not to procrastinate when this happens—you will only delay the celebrations.

Some faculties require an oral exam or *viva voce*, during which you will be asked questions on aspects of your research findings, methodology, interpretation of the data, reading and so on. The main aim is to satisfy the examiners that you have a good understanding of your research topic (which you will have after so much work!) so stay confident. The section on presenting a research project (p. 58–60) will help with this aspect.

GETTING THE BEST FROM SUPERVISION

When supervision works well the whole research process is made easier and less stressful for all concerned. To get the best out of your supervision you should begin by choosing your supervisor carefully. Investigate who stands out as a person who knows your research area well. Try to attend seminars by potential supervisors to get a feel for their approach and suitability. Make an appointment to discuss your ideas and each other's expectations. It is also a good idea to check that person's time constraints. It is no use choosing a guru in the field if that person is always too busy to supervise you adequately. If you are a distance student, check on your supervisor's experience and willingness to work in such a mode. E-mail and other online tools may be used for frequent communication. A preliminary meeting will give you a sense of how well you will be able to work with each other—personality plays a big part in the research process. Basically you need to get on with each other. In some cases, particularly for a PhD course, you may have both a main and an associate supervisor, each with expertise that complements your research objectives.

There are three key strategies that will ensure that research studies go well from the outset:

- Set out a timetable of regular meetings for the semester or year; distance students can undertake these through online tools such as chat facilities or video conferencing.
- Find a mentor in the workplace with whom you can discuss study and process issues.
- After each meeting with your supervisor, summarise the main points in an e-mail so that you both have a running record of what has been discussed. Divide the notes into four sections: research directions to follow; people to contact; resources to access, and other issues discussed.

STAYING ON TRACK

These hints will help you to get prepared and stay on track during research studies.

- Set up important tools such as a computer and main software early in the course.
- Prepare yourself by learning to use the computer tools you will need, whether it is a word processing or database program, a bibliographic tool, e-mail or Internet researching skills. Your institution will run courses on these topics, so check with the postgraduate association.
- Brush up on your academic skills by doing a course on thesis writing, researching techniques, research methodology or statistics. Check with the student learning support unit or the postgraduate association on when such courses are offered.
- Book yourself in for a library tour for research students and become familiar with library resources.
- Back up your work on the computer as you go along. Things do go wrong and material can be permanently lost, so get into the habit of making copies of your work and labelling each disk appropriately. The postgraduate centre, library or student

labs may have a zip drive you can use if you have to save substantial amounts of information.

- Organise a set yearly schedule of appointments with your supervisor so that you are assured of regular assistance and can use your time effectively between appointments.
- Have a realistic time-management plan.
- Keep writing! Once you start it is important to keep up the creativity and the motivation levels. Even on days when you feel a little low it is important to do some writing, say 800–1000 words.
- Avoid excessive use of jargon. Jargon is hard to omit in certain fields of study which depend on it more than others. Use it only when unavoidable and make sure you understand the meaning of each term.
- Reading successful research studies in your discipline will give you an idea of how the better ones are set out and argued. These documents are usually kept in the library. Ask your supervisor to point out those worth reading.

The devising and writing up of a research project should be carefully planned and executed. Your lecturer will be of assistance in directing your reading and questioning processes—in fact, at postgraduate level the relationship between supervisor and student is often one of collaboration.

> **Wisdom is the principal thing; therefore get wisdom: and with all thy getting get understanding.**
>
> *Proverbs 4:7*

12

Using technology

Using web-based tools is exciting as they can often provide access to large sources of information. Nonetheless, it is easy to waste time and allow yourself to be distracted by all that is on offer. Technology is a useful learning tool when used wisely. Technological tools include the Internet, electronic databases, word processors, electronic journals, online library catalogues, e-mail, chat and discussion lists. This chapter looks at their effective use.

THE INTERNET

The Internet (or Net) has become a complicated worldwide network in the relatively short time of its history. The Internet started from a project begun by the US Defence Department in the 1960s to design a computer network that would be able to continue operating in the case of a nuclear attack, even if part of it was destroyed. The project was extended in the 1970s to include American research and academic organisations in order to share information. The rest is technology history. Nowadays all sorts of academic information is available via the Internet which, when used wisely, can be a valuable scholarly tool. It offers access to a range of information including media, newspaper reports, library catalogues, financial and statistical data, government documents, online journal articles and other web-based publications. The Internet allows you to communicate with people both at your institution and outside it through e-mail, chat and discussion lists.

SEARCHING AND RESEARCHING ONLINE

Searching for information is easier and more efficient when you have a clear idea of what you are actually searching for. This might seem like a trivial statement but when you are challenged constantly by new ideas and theories it is easy to stray from the actual goal. This is particularly true of online searching, where you are bombarded with information. To find information on the Web you can start with a specific site or do a general search using a search engine, a tool that will look up and present a list of sites in response to the key word or topic that you type in. It is up to you to examine the value of these sites, which can turn into a time-consuming task. The trick to online searching is to compare results from a number of search engines; some are better than others in linking you to relevant information in your discipline area.

Analysing your topic

Analyse your topic to identify what information will actually help you. Brainstorm the issues, perhaps on a piece of paper that you pin above your desk for easy reference. Consider the key words that identify or describe your topic; for writer's block, for instance, you might list 'writing anxiety', 'writing style' or 'writing apprehension'.

Search engines

To access the World Wide Web (WWW) you need to select an online search engine such as Yahoo (http://yahoo.com) or Altavista (http://altavista.com). To see which search engine is likely to provide the best results for your purposes, compare the number of sites each has found on your topic. Appendix 1 has a list of search engines for you to try.

Analysing an information source for validity

Critically analyse your information, particularly the information you get from the Internet. Unlike books, which go through a screening procedure before publication, documents can be published on the Web by anyone. You may need to invest some time reviewing the source and the value of the document. For example, a commercial company with a vested interest might have put a particular document on the Web; it is likely to have a biased point of view. Figure 12.1 provides guidelines for evaluating search engine results.

Figure 12.1 Evaluating search engine results

- How many hits came up on your screen overall?
- How many of these were for books or other commercial services?
- How many hits seem to be valid or relevant?
- Is the information the most recent?
- Is the information valid (that is, devised by dependable sources/ authorities)?
- Do the sites contain helpful or relevant visuals?
- Do the sites link to other relevant sites?

When a WWW search fails

Sometimes searches fail as a result of technical problems, the Web address has changed with no connecting link to the new address provided, or because of human error. First check the address—it is easy to omit something or type in a wrong word or symbol. If the address is correct, try typing in chunks of the web address to get to the home page. Working backwards is usually the most effective way to do this; for example, with the address:

http://osiris.sunderland.ac.uk/rif/w3searches.all/sym.html

you would eliminate the last chunk:

http://osiris.sunderland.ac.uk/rif/w3searches.all/

and if necessary the next chunk. If there is a glitch somewhere and you are still unsuccessful, try again in another day or two.

Losing your sense of direction

Occasionally it happens that following a line of thinking away from your original plan can lead to a goldmine of ideas and information, but it more often leads to a dead end and lots of wasted time. Searches can be undertaken by author, title, subject or key word and by adding a 'limiting word'. You can customise searches. For example, a search on *heart disease* might be done as:

heart and disease and effects (or *heart + disease + effects* or '*heart disease effects*')

Your search results will include the three terms. If you wanted to concentrate on the effects of heart disease on men you could limit your search by doing:

heart + disease + effects + men

or you could use *not* to exclude a category, in this case women:

heart + disease + effects not women

(though this search might give you men, children and animals).

Using an asterisk (*) will call up any related words, for instance,

managing* + heart + disease

will automatically include terms such as *management, manage, manageable, manageability* (of heart disease).

For a wide search of issues on both the management and effects of heart disease use the combination:

heart + disease + effects or management*

EVALUATING WEBSITE VALIDITY

Remember that the Internet is a user-beware system: no one is responsible for it, thus there may be no editing process, checking of facts or keeping a document or site up to date. While those who place information on the Web are responsible for their site, it does not necessarily follow that the site is a responsible one: its information could be out of date, biased, of poor quality or untrue. It is essential to review the information received over the Web critically. A lecturer may ask you to present an evaluation of a website; the purpose of this assignment is to get you thinking critically about the validity of mass-distributed information in your discipline. Some of the things you should consider include the relevance and authority of the information (is it up-to-date and referenced correctly?), navigational aspects (can you find your way around the site easily?), and general presentation (is the information easy to read, and is the site attractive?).

ELECTRONIC JOURNALS

Online journals (generally known as electronic journals or e-journals) are another valuable source of information. Some are available free of charge, others have a subscription cost. Before you spend money on a subscription, check whether you can access the journal in paper format, through the university library or the inter-library loan system. If the library has subscribed to the journal for its staff and students, all you need is a password. Websites for e-journals usually indicate the contents of each publication; some also include complete articles. Sites where you can find out which e-journals are relevant to your discipline include:

Internet Public Library	http://www.ipl.org/reading/serials
E-journal directories	http://www.aph.gov.au/library/ intguide/gen/genjrnl.html
UnCover	http://uncweb.carl.org

DATABASES

In addition to print-based and microfiche databases, there are online versions that you can access through the Web and others in CD-ROM format. These are all discipline-specific. Your lecturer or librarian can tell you which are relevant to your field and point out their specific search functions. Online databases are available through passwords so find out from your librarian how to register. The library's CD-ROM collection can be accessed via computer (again with a password). Online databases are updated quite frequently, while CD-ROM databases are current only up to the date of publication. Index and abstract databases are available for many disciplines, so check with your lecturer or librarian for any that might be useful. New ones are published frequently. You can search databases by author, title, subject area and even specify dates.

COMMUNICATING ONLINE

As technology becomes increasingly integrated into tertiary level studies, online communication through e-mail, discussion lists and chat systems is becoming more widely used. Discussion lists and e-mail have some advantages over spontaneous or real-time conversation—they allow you to think before you initiate or respond to communication, allow you to express yourself in written form rather than orally (this might suit the learning styles of some students) and facilitate communication for shy people uncomfortable with face-to-face communication. Common courtesies apply to online communication; this is sometimes termed *netiquette*. *Flaming* (offensive or distasteful comments, brash or harsh putdowns) is not acceptable. You need to bring it to the attention of the subject lecturer if it occurs.

Discussion lists or bulletin boards

Subject lecturers often set up discussion lists or bulletin boards for their classes; you might find others of interest as well. Discussion can revolve around study topics, readings and study issues. In the case of subject-organised lists, lecturers quite often sit back and watch or even assess online interaction. Discussion lists work best when there is an actual discussion rather than just a series of quick questions and answers. Active participation in discussion lists means picking up on an issue that is presented (or presenting one yourself) and writing up some of your critical thinking for others to comment on, extend and develop. If your lecturer assesses participation on the class discussion list, it is this type of interaction which demonstrates your learning. While participating passively or lurking (reading rather than adding to the discussion) is also appropriate, consider taking an active role at times to further develop your understanding of an issue and your online communication skills. There is practical merit to participating actively, as it can allow a lecturer to gauge the level of participation of students not physically sitting in class.

Your lecturer should be able to advise you on general discussion lists for your particular discipline. You can also check whether relevant associations have discussion list links on their home pages. Discussion lists can be very helpful as they allow you to post questions you are investigating, get feedback on certain perspectives or ideas, and make contact with others working in your research area.

Using chat facilities

Online chat systems (chat rooms/chat lines) differ from discussion lists in that they allow you to communicate spontaneously or in real time. (Students usually enjoy this facility because they can forget about grammar and spelling for a time!) Using chat you may communicate with a group or move into another space/room to 'talk' on a one-to-one basis. You can arrange suitable times for discussions, which are more like face-to-face conversations than communication in discussion lists, which tends to be more focused. Your lecturer may know of discipline-oriented chat rooms that could be of value to your studies. Various associations may have chat room links on their home pages.

Hints on getting the most out of discussion lists and chat systems appear in Figure 12.2.

Figure 12.2 Using discussion lists or chat rooms effectively

- Participate in the list just as you would in a tutorial—ask questions, comment, ask for clarification, etc.
- Don't feel embarrassed or shy about participating. Your ideas or questions will trigger responses which can only result in creative discussion. The ideas that come out of your discussions will help develop your critical thinking on a topic.
- Word your contributions clearly and courteously.

- Don't post test messages as they break up a line of discussion and are annoying; you will soon find out if your messages don't come through.
- Check the discussion lists or chat frequently, perhaps as often as you check your e-mail.

Communicating via electronic mail (e-mail)

In many universities research students are allocated an e-mail address on enrolment in the course and provided with instructions on how to receive and send messages.

Figure 12.3 gives pointers for using e-mail efficiently as part of your studies.

Figure 12.3 Using e-mail effectively

- Ensure you have an e-mail address and know how to use the system as part of your course.
- Check your e-mail regularly but do not substitute it for real work. Using e-mail can be a great time-waster.
- Do something with your e-mail as you open it. Either store it, respond to it or trash it so you don't end up with a long and confusing list of out-of-date communications.
- Write a short, relevant message in the subject line so the recipient knows immediately what the e-mail is about.
- Make your message clear, and get to the point quickly and courteously.
- Prioritise your e-mail, particularly if it's important. E-mail can be sent with a *high, normal,* or *low* priority tag attached; this helps the recipient prioritise messages when time is short, and can ensure that your message is not lost in a sea of mail.
- Some lecturers specify times for collecting and responding to messages; it pays to have a record of this.

USING A WORD PROCESSOR

Each of us has a different approach to using the word processor as a writing tool. As we become more familiar with it, our approach to writing changes also. Many students start off drafting on paper and using the word processor only for writing up. As they become more proficient with the word processor, they may plan with pen and paper and develop this material on screen, some even moving rapidly to planning on-screen as well. The advantages of the word processor are that the editing and drafting processes are simplified as there is no need to write up the whole text with each new draft, there is a spell-check function so that you can get on with the writing task, and the finished product is presentable and easy to read. It is a good investment of skills to learn to use a word processor efficiently. As you develop your skills you will find that the word processor no longer inhibits your thinking or writing; you may end up drafting directly on-screen. Reading and navigating on-screen will become easier also.

A few words of warning. Firstly, get into the habit of saving your work every ten minutes and backing up at the end of every session. Secondly, do not treat the grammar check as infallible—this function cannot take into account style and context, and regularly presents inappropriate responses. Lastly, do not be concerned with what the word processor can do, rather concentrate on what you want it to do.

Technology offers exciting aids to study, allowing us to access information, manipulate it and present it in paper or electronic formats. However, technology also means that we may be presented with too much information, often of dubious quality, to wade through. It is worth taking time to learn how to use technology efficiently so that it enhances your learning rather than leading you astray along the paths of electronic wizardry.

Appendices

1. USEFUL RESOURCES

USEFUL TEXT SOURCES

Academic skills

De Fazio, T. 1999, *Studying in Australia: A guide for international students*, Allen & Unwin, Sydney.

Fairburn, G. J. & Winch, C. 1996, *Reading, Writing and Reasoning: A guide for students*, Open University Press, Buckingham.

Germov, J. & Williams, L. 1999, *Get Great Information Fast*, Allen & Unwin, Sydney.

Marshall, L. & Rowland, F. 1998, *A Guide to Learning Independently*, 3rd edn, Longman, Melbourne.

Wallace, A., Schirato, T. & Bright, P. 1999, *Beginning University: Thinking, researching and writing for success*, Allen & Unwin, Sydney.

Writing

Anderson, J. & Poole, M. 1998, *Assignment and Thesis Writing*, John Wiley & Sons, Brisbane.

Bate, D. & Sharpe, S. 1996, *Writer's Handbook: For university students*, Harcourt Brace, Sydney.

Emerson, L. & McPherson, J. (eds) 1997, *Writing Guidelines for Education Students*, Dunmore Press, New Zealand.

Germov, J. 2000, *Get Great Marks for Your Essays*, 2nd edn, Allen & Unwin, Sydney.

Osland, D., Boyd, D., McKenna, W. & Salusinszky, I. 1991, *Writing in Australia: A composition course for tertiary students*, Harcourt Brace Jovanovich, Sydney.

Research projects

Anderson, J. & Poole, M. 1994, *Thesis and Assignment Writing*, 3rd edn, Jacaranda Wiley, Brisbane.

Bell, J. 1999, *Doing Your Research Project: A guide for first-time researchers in Education and Social Science*, 3rd edn, Open University Press, Milton Keynes.

Day, R. 1995, *How to Write and Publish a Scientific Paper*, 4th edn, Cambridge University Press.

Evans, D. 1995, *How to Write a Better Thesis or Report*, Melbourne University Press, Melbourne.

Phillips, E. M. & Pugh, D. S. 1994, *How to Get a PhD: A handbook for students and their supervisors*, 2nd edn, Open University Press, Milton Keynes.

Referencing

American Psychological Association 1994, *Publication Manual of the American Psychological Association*, 4th edn, American Psychological Association, Washington, DC.

——2000, *Electronic reference formats recommended by the American Psychological Association*, [Web document], http://www.apa.org.journals/webref.html (date accessed 11 January 2001).

Li, X. & Crane, N. 1993, *Electronic Style: A guide to citing information*, Meckler, Westport.

MLA Handbook for Writers of Research Papers 1995, 4th edn, Gibaldi, J. MLA, New York.
Style Manual for Authors, Editors and Printers 2001, 6th edn, Australian Government Publishing Service, Canberra.

ELECTRONIC RESOURCES

Electronic journals

http://www.ipl.org/reading/serials	Internet Public Library
http://uncweb.carl.org	UnCover

Searching on the WWW

General searches can be undertaken using any of the following search engines:

Altavista	http://altavista.com
Excite	http://www.excite.com
Google	http://www.google.com
Hotbot	http://www.hotbot.com
Infoseek	http://infoseek.com
Looksmart	http://www.looksmart.com
Lycos	http://www.lycos.com
Yahoo	http://yahoo.com

The following use a number of search engines in one search:

Metacrawler	http://www.go2net.com/search.html
Metafind	http://www.metafind.com
Savvysearch	http://www.savvysearch.com
W3 Search engines	http://osiris.sunderland.ac.uk/rif/w3 searches

These directories can be used for subject-specific searches:

Ask Jeeves	http://www.askjeeves.com
Encyclopedia Britannica Internet Guide	http://www.eblast.com
Lycos	http://www.lycos.com
The Argus Clearinghouse	http://www.clearinghouse.com.net
WWW Virtual Library	http://www.w3.org/vl
Yahoo	http://yahoo.com

2. EXAMPLE OF CRITERIA FOR ASSESSING ORAL PRESENTATIONS

	Excellent	Very good	Good	Pass	Poor
Structure • focused on topic • logical structure • moved from one main point to another smoothly • presented as a team (if applicable)					
Content • introduction clear • main ideas clear • relevant support material • conclusion clear • important points covered • relevant material • used no repetition • used other sources appropriately					
Style • confident presentation • appropriate speaking pace • audible • eye contact					
Visual or other aids • clear visuals • visuals not crowded with information • aids relevant to presentation					
Overall • well prepared • clearly presented • easy to follow					

3. COMMON NOTE-TAKING ABBREVIATIONS

i.e.	that is
→	leads to
@	at
+	and
e.g.	example
≈	approximately
n/no.	number
min	minimum
max	maximum
sub	subject
bk	book
info	inform/information
imp	important
gov	govern/government
u/s	understand/understanding
>	greater than
<	less than
v.	very
w	with
w/o	without
b/c	because

4. REFERENCES RECORD SHEET

Subject _____

Author surname	Author initials	Date published	Title	Publisher	Place	Pages	Document type	Date accessed	Call no.	Comments on content

5. COMMONLY USED INSTRUCTION WORDS

Analyse/ examine	Break the subject into components and write about how these parts relate to each other, whether there any tensions. You need to look at *how* and *why*.
Account for	Explain why something occurs, provide reasons.
Contrast/ compare	Present similarities and differences between two issues, events, procedures, phenomena, works and so on. Identify some aspects of, for instance, two works of literature and see how each of these aspects is dealt with in each work. Don't try to write about too many aspects. Dealing with two or three thoroughly is better than dealing with five or six superficially.
Discuss/ comment	Note down the various aspects relating to a topic and why these are of interest to people in your field of study. Try not to bring too many points into your essay. Include your point of view on these aspects and supporting evidence. Focus on major aspects, particularly if you have a small word limit.
Describe/ explain	Talk about the facts or an event or a process. You don't need to interpret, just point out main issues or aspects.
Evaluate	Consider a text, a theory, an approach, a situation, and make your own judgement of its strengths and weaknesses.
Illustrate	Clarify something (situation, argument, etc.).
Interpret	Explain something (situation, reasons, argument, logic, etc.), showing relevance or meaning.
Justify	Explain reasons behind something or a situation (a decision, an argument or idea), provide information on rationale.

Outline	Present the main points of an issue in an ordered or sequenced way.
Review	Examine, analyse and interpret the main issues relating to a topic.
Summarise	Present the main ideas of a text, argument, idea, approach or procedure. Details are not included.
Trace	Demonstrate the sequence or order of an argument, situation, process or event.

6. CONNECTIVES OR CONJUNCTIONS

Expressing different points of view

in contrast	however	although	in spite of
in comparison	but	nevertheless	besides
on the contrary	yet	nonetheless	alternatively
on the other hand	though	despite	or

Expressing time
prior
before
after
afterwards
meanwhile

Joining ideas

firstly	in addition
secondly	additionally
thirdly	moreover
finally	further
also	furthermore
again	then

Similar points of view
equally
likewise
similarly
accordingly
in addition

Expressing results
thus
therefore
so
consequently
hence
as a result

Explaining
for example
for instance
that is
in other words
in particular

Clarifying
in other words
to reiterate
in essence
briefly

Expressing importance
above all
significantly
an important
more importantly
in fact
importantly

Concluding
to sum up
in summary
in short
to conclude
in conclusion
in brief
in other words

7. WEEKLY STUDY SCHEDULE

Time	Monday	Tuesday	Wednesday	Thursday	Friday	Saturday	Sunday
8.00–9.00							
9.00–10.00							
10.00–11.00							
11.00–12.00							
12.00–1.00							
1.00–2.00							
2.00–3.00							
3.00–4.00							
4.00–5.00							
5.00–6.00							
6.00–7.00							
7.00–8.00							
8.00–9.00							
9.00–10.00							

8. SEMESTER STUDY SCHEDULE

	Subject:	Subject:	Subject:
Week 1			
Week 2			
Week 3			
Week 4			
Week 5			
Week 6			
Week 7			
Week 8			
Week 9			
Week 10			
Week 11			
Week 12			
Week 13			

Glossary

abstract	A synthesis of the main points presented in the essay/report/thesis, etc.
appendix	Section of a text that contains information additional to that presented in the body of the text, such as a chart, table, graph, questionnaire. It appears at the end of the document.
bibliography	List of resources used by a writer in preparing a text.
brainstorming	Spontaneous thinking and listing/discussion of ideas.
browser	Program (such as Netscape, Lynx, Internet Explorer) that reads documents on the Internet. This program selects documents and goes from one document to another.
chat (chat rooms, chat lines)	Space where spontaneous communication takes place over the Internet.
connectives	Words and phrases used to link ideas so that they assist the flow of an argument.
copyright law	Law which dictates that only a certain amount of a text may be copied as a single copy for individual use. It does not permit copying parts of a text nor making multiple

	copies without obtaining special permission from the publisher and/or copyright holder first.
cross-reference	An indication of a link between one point in the text and another (usually a page or chapter reference).
discipline	An area of study. Recognised disciplines include health, business, engineering, education, law.
discussion lists	Communication centred around a theme or topic that occurs over the Net. It can be viewed at a particular address or you can participate in it through your e-mail account.
dissertation	*see* thesis.
e-mail	Abbreviation for Electronic Mail. This program allows you to receive and send messages over the Internet.
EndNote	Program that allows you to record bibliographic information and additional notes relating to a resource.
'hits'	(Internet term) Refers to the number of matches to your search request.
home page	The first page on a website, seen as the welcome or title page. A home page usually includes an index of other pages linked to the site.
hyperlink	Link on a WWW site that allows you to go from one site to another. For example, you can click on a word or visual which takes you to a related site on the Web. Links are normally presented in a different colour and/or underlined so they stand out from the text, and the cursor changes to a hand symbol when it is over a link.

instruction word	Word or term that details what is required from a question, for instance, the word 'explain'.
Internet (or Net)	Collection of interconnected computer networks that exchange information through a telecommunications system.
journal	Periodical publication presenting information on a particular discipline.
login	The account name that allows you to access a computer system.
mindmap	A visual representation of ideas which indicates the relationships between them and can be used for visualising information or planning assignments.
modem	Piece of hardware that connects your computer to others through a telephone line.
netiquette	Term made up from the words 'etiquette' and 'the NET', and used to describe rules of common courtesy when communicating via the Internet.
OHT	Overhead transparency.
paraphrase	To 'use other words', for instance, in a summary or an indirect quote.
password	Code used to access a secure system; you may have a password to access your e-mail so that it can only be viewed by you.
plagiarism	Using another person's ideas or words and presenting them as one's own.
postgraduate	Refers to a course that follows on from undergraduate courses, or a student who has completed an undergraduate course and continues to higher-level studies.

reference	Information that indicates an original source, and includes author, title and publishing details.
referencing system	Particular convention that outlines how referencing details should be presented.
search engine	Used to access information on the Internet (similar to a catalogue system).
synopsis	Brief summary of a written text such as an essay, report or presentation.
thesis	Lengthy research paper usually written as part of postgraduate level study in a Masters or Doctoral degree.
thesis statement	Statement which outlines the main idea of a thesis.
topic sentence	Details the main idea of a paragraph.
transcript	Official record of a student's study progress.
undergraduate	Refers to a bachelor degree or first level studies at tertiary level, or a student undertaking such studies.
URL	Abbreviation for Uniform Resources Locator which acts as an Internet address so that the Internet browser knows where to locate a site.
WWW	Abbreviation commonly used to indicate the World Wide Web. The Web is a collection of many linked resources (audio, visual, text, animation) that can be transmitted via computer.

References

American Psychological Association 1994, *Publication Manual of the American Psychological Association,* 4th edn, American Psychological Association, Washington, DC.

——2000 *Electronic reference formats recommended by the American Psychological Association,* [Web document], http://www.apa.org.journals/webref.html (date accessed 11 January 2001).

Brown, H. D. 1994, *Teaching by Principles: An interactive approach to language pedagogy,* Prentice-Hall, New Jersey.

Elbow, P. 1981, *Writing with Power: Techniques for mastering the writing process,* Oxford University Press, New York.

Gardner, H. 1993, *Frames of Mind: Theory of multiple intelligences,* Basic Books, New York.

Jensen, G. M. & Di Tiberio, J. K. 1989, *Personality and the Teaching of Composition,* Ablex Publishing Co., Norwood, New Jersey.

Li, X. & Crane, N. 1993, *Electronic Style: A guide to citing information,* Meckler, Westport.

Style Manual for Authors, Editors and Printers, 1988, 5th edn, Australian Government Publishing Service, Canberra.

Index

5008037R0

Made in the USA
Lexington, KY
24 March 2010